HIGH HOPES FOR THE CHURCH

Biblical expectations for God's people

BILLIE KESSNER FRIEL

BROADMAN PRESS
Nashville, Tennessee

ISBN: 0-8054-5084-X
Dewey Decimal Classification: 262.7
Subject Heading: CHURCH
Library of Congress Catalog Card Number: 89-35755

Printed in the United States of America

Library of Congress Cataloging-in-Publication Data
Friel, Billie Kessner, 1946-
    High hopes for the Church / Billie Kessner Friel.
        p.   cm.
    ISBN 0-8054-5084-X
    1. Church--Biblical teaching. 2. Bible. N.T. Epistles of
Paul-Criticism, interpretation, etc. 3. Christian life—Baptist
authors. I. Title.
BS2655.C5F75 1990
262—dc20
                                                            89-35755
                                                            CIP

Dedication

My first book is dedicated to my
First Family
Marilynn, beloved wife (Prov. 31:10)
My beloved children (Ps. 127:3-5)
Christa, Laura, and Daniel

Preface

How can the church of the Lord Jesus Christ experience comfort in crisis?

How can the church gracefully handle church conflict?

How can the church prepare to face the Judgment Seat of Christ?

In my lifetime, I have been a member of only five churches, three of which I have served as pastor. I accepted Christ in a small Central Florida congregation. During my first two years of college, I belonged to a dynamic, soul-winning fellowship. During my last two years of college, I held my initial pastorate. During seminary days, I was pastor of a church near the Mississippi River in South Louisiana. I have been at my present congregation, the First Baptist Church of Mount Juliet, Tennessee, since 1972. All of these churches were victorious. Yes, I have *High Hopes for the Church*!

Throughout my ministry I have been attracted to the Pauline Epistles because of Paul's honesty in describing and facing every conceivable church situation. In this book I range throughout the apostle's letters, even though I do pay particular attention to the church at Corinth. The Corinthian church, for instance, was one of Paul's greatest crowns--but also one of his greatest crosses. There were revivals and riots. He had front-door and back-door revivals. In all of these situations--many of which seemed hopeless and impossible--Paul never lost his high hopes for the church!

The themes of this book revolve around the purpose and process of how the church can obtain comfort even amid crises; the "inward man" and how to stay strong in the Lord, how to handle church conflict, the measure of a church's giving; the activity of the devil against the church; the evidences of Christ in one's life; the fragrance of the gospel in a foul-smelling world; the Bema or Judgment Seat of Christ; our spiritual warfare; the "thorn in the flesh"; and facts about our Lord's second coming.

Yes, Paul had high hopes for the church. Admittedly, many are giving up on the church today, but they are mistaken. More than ever I firmly believe in the church: its Founder, its foundation, and its future. She may leak, but she will never sink! The issues with which Paul grappled are as up-to-date as tomorrow's newspaper.

Every believer should heed the Word of God concerning hope for the church in a hopeless world.

Contents

1
Comfort in Crises

2 Corinthians 1:3-7

Preaching has been described as "saying things people don't understand about subjects which are of no concern!" No one could have accused the apostle Paul of that kind of preaching. In this text the apostle deals with two of his favorite themes: trouble and comfort. No less than six times in verses 3-11 of 2 Corinthians 1 do we encounter the noun and verb forms of comfort.

Out of the thirteen chapters in 2 Corinthians, these subjects are discovered in five of them. Paul does not speak in a language people do not understand about irrelevant subjects! His teaching is as up-to-date as tomorrow morning's newspaper.

A woman had been grieving over her dead son for a long time. Finally, she went to a wise man for counsel. He told her, "I will give you back your son if you will bring me some mustard seed. The only stipulation is that the mustard seed must be from a home where there has never been any sorrow." The woman left and searched everywhere. She returned with the confession, "How selfish I've been in my grief. Sorrow is common to all."

Because sorrow and comfort are common to all, it is crucial that we explore God's Word about these deep concerns. Let me nail down four principles from the text.

Occurrence of Crises

Just as "comfort" is mentioned often here, so is the thought of crises. For instance, count the number of times "tribulation," "trouble," or "affliction" are mentioned in this passage. Paul uses two Greek words to describe crises:

1. *Thlipsis* is translated "tribulation" (v. 4), "trouble" (v. 4), and "affliction" (v. 6). It is an often-used word for tribulation, trouble, and distress. It literally means painful pressure or a burden beneath a heavy weight. A loaded-down wagon or truck aptly describes this term.

2. *Patheema* is translated "sufferings" in verses 5, 6, and 7. We derive our word *pathos* from the same root--*paschein.* The word also refers to the sufferings of Christ—His passion. Years ago I heard a sermon that stuck with me concerning the occurrence of crises. It was based on 1 Peter 4:12: "Beloved, think it not strange concerning the fiery trial which is to try you, as though some strange thing happened unto you." Think it not strange! Trouble, tribulation, and affliction will assuredly enter our lives. Do not think it unusual when they hit us.

Basically, there are three types of crises into which all troubles fall. We have trouble because of three key relationships:

1. *We Are Related to the Natural World*—do you remember the results of Adam's sin? The man, woman, serpent, and the creation were cursed (see Gen. 3:14-19). Since the fall, all of creation—the natural world—has been in bondage to corruption (Rom. 8:21). Because human beings are related to the natural world, they receive trouble from three sources:

A. *Destruction*—There are natural catastrophes over which humans have no control. Trouble plagues human

life as we experience the destruction of hurricanes, torna-
does, cyclones, tidal waves, earthquakes, and other devastating natural events. These disasters have often been
called "acts of God." My wife and I were personally involved in the obliteration produced by Hurricane Camille
in South Louisiana. Humanity had no choice but to brace
itself against that natural catastrophe. Indescribable
tribulation, affliction, and trouble wrecked the lives of
thousands of people.

B. *Death*—Because one is related to the natural world,
one must face the crisis of death. The death rate has never changed: one death for every birth! "For as in Adam all
die, even so in Christ shall all be made alive" (1 Cor.
15:22). The grim reaper has affected the peace and tran-
quillity of us all.

C. *Disease*—Sickness falls over our lives and causes
suffering. Each of us has been affected by this result of
corruption in the natural world. *Cancer* is one of the most
feared words in our vocabulary! Horrid germs abound,
even in this day of advanced medical technology. As we
live in the natural world, we have all manner of trouble
and tribulation because of disease.

A mother once dressed her son in his uniform before his
first football game and instructed, "Now, Son, try not to
get dirty or injured!" Isn't that like some mothers? Once
that boy puts on his uniform and steps onto the playing
field, he will certainly get dirty and might well get hurt.
As humans, in the game of life, we will certainly get dirty
and injured if we live long enough. Destruction, death,
and disease will impact our daily existence.

2. *We Are Related to the World of People*—Many of our

troubles come because of our interaction with other people. The sinful nature is in all of us. We may have personality conflicts with other people. Anger wells up in us
when we feel our rights are being threatened.

Think of the disappointments you've had through relationships with people: misunderstandings, hurt feelings,
rejections, breaking of covenants, and, possibly, even a
marriage breakup. The Psalms are full of references to
problems caused by people. None are so vivid as David's
remembrance in Psalm 55:12-14:

> For it was not an enemy that reproached me; then I could
> have borne it: neither was it he that hated me that did
> magnify himself against me; then I would have hid myself
> from him: But it was thou, a man mine equal, my guide,
> and mine acquaintance. We took sweet counsel together,
> walked unto the house of God in company.

We remember that our Lord was betrayed by one of His
disciples, and His own countrymen were partly respon-
sible for putting Him on the cross. We will have a variety
of afflictions and troubles because we are related to the
human race.

3. *We Are Related to Christ*. This is the only type of
trouble in our lives over which we have a choice! When we
make the choice to receive Christ, a new form of crisis will
rear its head: persecution.

Jesus spoke often of the inevitable persecution of His
followers. In John 15:18-21, Christ emphasized that the
world would hate us because it hated Him. Because we
are not of the evil world system, we will be persecuted.
Who can forget the memorable Beatitude in Matthew
5:10-12? Everyone loves to hear the first seven blessings
upon the children of God. However, the eighth Beatitude

declares the certain occurrence of persecution for those who choose to make Jesus Savior and Lord.

Paul presented a vivid case for the certain occurrence of trouble because of one's relationship to Christ. Notice in 2 Corinthians 11:23-33 the extensive list of tribulations endured by Paul: beatings, imprisonments, stonings, shipwreck, and multiple perils.

A visiting evangelist was asked by the church's pastor to lead in prayer. As they sat on the platform during the opening music, the pastor pointed out needs in the congregation. "That little lady in the back just lost her husband. The couple to your right has a son who ran away from home this week. The pretty woman in the second row had her husband to leave her recently." The pastor continued to give sentence descriptions of congregational needs. By the time the evangelist walked to the pulpit to pray, he was brokenhearted! In all of our lives and experiences, there is the sure occurrence of crises.

Origin of Comfort

What and where is the source of true comfort? Paul erupts in a doxology of praise in 2 Corinthians 1:3 to the "God of all comfort." The only true origin of comfort for this world's crises is the Triune God--the Father, the Son, and the Holy Spirit.

How does the world attempt to find comfort? Usually, a kind of escapism characterizes the world's search for comfort. Alcohol and drugs are forms of escape as the person drinks or uses "dope" trying to forget his problems. However, problems cannot be drowned--they float! Unless the alcohol or drug abuser dies, he will eventually have to come down from his "buzz" or "high" and face his problems again! People sometimes think a good night's sleep can transport them away from their problems. However, even a peace-promising posturepedic mattress can never supply sleep to a troubled heart. The world tries escape as the pathway to comfort, but people cannot escape a tormented conscience or gnawing inward guilt.

Genuine comfort comes only from God. Only Jesus could declare and truly mean it: "Let not your heart be troubled: ye believe in God, believe also in me" (John 14:1). Our Master soothes a troubled world: "Come unto me, all ye that labour and are heavy laden, and I will give you rest" (Matt. 11:28).

How does God comfort us? Let me count a few ways:

1. *The Scriptures*—*T*he Word of God soothes and strengthens the troubled heart. Faith comes by hearing the Word of God (Rom. 10:17). Once my family was facing a critical surgery. The night before the operation was unforgettable as God gave us a word from *His Word* the Bible. We *could* enter that anxious situation the *following* day with comfort *and* sustenance in our hearts.

2. *Sympathetic Ministries of Friends*—*T*hose in the family of God, the believers, have repeatedly experienced the sweet comfort ministered to them by their brothers in the faith. "A friend loveth at all times" (Prov. 17:17). A call, a card, or a visit can make a difference during a time of need. Often just our being there is so therapeutic for the bereaved at the funeral home. In many cases, human words simply will not suffice. What a ministry we can offer those in and out of the fellowship of faith!

3. *Removal of Affliction*—We have a great God! Nothing is too hard for our Heavenly Father. Sometimes God will remove the affliction. I shall never forget the first ministry of healing in which I had a part. A godly lady had the dread disease lupus and had gradually become worse. One evening several of us sat around her bed.

Her husband observed, "You know, we've prayed about

Sandy for years. We've made room for lupus in our lives. Why don't we pray that God will take it away?" We did exactly that. I have never heard such intense praying. My faith was not the reason she was healed, but, as we prayed, an inexpressible sense of God's presence permeated her sick room. The husband and wife seemed to be in perfect accord as they prayed together. They were convinced that God had performed a miracle. The following day the doctors were asked to test Sandy once again. They found no trace of the disease--and seventeen years later, the lupus is still gone. God can remove the affliction from our lives.

4. *The Holy Spirit's Ministry*—Jesus told us in John 14:16 and 18 of the coming Holy Spirit who would be the great Comforter. As a matter of fact, the word used for the six occ*urrences of* "comfort" in 2 Corinthians 1:3-11 is the same word used to describe the Comforter in John 14:16. "Comforter" ("Paraclete") is apt to describe the Holy Spirit's ministry as He comes alongside the one in grief. An expressive picture of a Paraclete appeared in the newspaper one year during football season. The team's quarterback had gone through a terrible game. The picture showed him leaning against the wall in the locker room. An assistant coach had his arm over the player's shoulder and was consoling him. When we stew in the cauldron of trials and troubles, we can be keenly aware of the Spirit's comforting ministry.

Opportunity of Crises

If you were to assist the caterpillar coming out of the cocoon, you'd kill it. If you helped the baby bird break through the shell, you'd be murdering the little fellow. Exertion at birth is needed by birds and insects. Through

God's providence we receive benefit through the crises of life. Let's examine a few results of our crises.

1. *They Test Our Faith*—First Peter 1:7 likens our faith to gold purified by the testings of fire. Do you really live and walk by faith? When we have our faith tested and tried, we learn the quality of our Christian experience. Sad to confess, many Christians don't have a faith strong enough to face the crises of life.

2. *They Produce Patience*—One of the profoundest needs of every person's life is patience, the grace dynamically to endure crises. Facing and overcoming crises through our faith produces patience, experience, and hope (Rom. 5:3,4). I remember when our first child contracted the croup. It terrified us new parents! We agonized over our little girl's health. Then the doctor recommended remedies for curing her croup: clear liquids, humidifier, steam from hot water in the bathroom, and wrapping her up and going outside. It was a different story the next time the croup came by our home! While we were concerned, we were not blown away by fear. Why? We had gone through the experience before and now had patience, experience, and hope. Facing crises produces patience.

3. *They Help Us Come to a New Place of Trust*—Notice in 2 Corinthians 1:9 the phrase, "We should not trust in ourselves, but in God which raiseth the dead." Crises have a way of stripping us of our self-confidence and putting our eyes on the Lord. How easy it is to become proud and self-reliant that we don't depend on our faith in God! Crises pull the rug from under us and force us once again to look up.

Romans 8:28 is still in the Book! "We know that all things work together for good to them that love God, to them who are the called according to his purpose." Notice that verse does not say, as many people mistakenly think, everything that happens is good—but everything can work together for good . . . "to them that love God . . ." In baking a cake, you would be disappointed if you taste each ingredient individually. But, taken together, the ingredients combine to make a delicious treat! We cannot see how God is mixing our experiences together. Every crisis affords an opportunity to do good for and in us. Before God can do anything *with* us, He must do something *in* us. Don't run from the crisis but learn all you can during it. What may seem terrible may actually be opportunity in disguise.

Obligation of Comfort

What have we learned so far? Namely, that crises will befall us because of our relationships to the natural world, the human world, and to Christ. God promises comfort in the crises, however. We must be alert to the opportunities of crises as God enrolls us in the school of "hard knocks" and affliction. Now, a marvelous principle emerges in 2 Corinthians 1:4—as we are comforted by God, we are obligated to share that comfort! Eureka! What a truth that only the Christian will understand!

Notice the progression in verse 4: God comforts us . . . the comfort we receive is passed on to others as we minister to them in their affliction. We become instruments of God, and through us He comforts those around us. We are stewards of all our experiences. Jesus taught, "Freely ye have received, freely give" (Matt. 10:8).

Imagine an ant carrying a massive—to her—piece of straw. The ant comes to a crack in the earth's surface over which she cannot cross by herself. However, she takes the straw in her mandibles, pushes it over the crack, and walks across the straw. The burden has become a bridge! In like manner, our burdens become literal bridges "over troubled water." We become conduits through whom comfort is dispensed. "For none of us liveth to himself, and no man dieth to himself" (Rom. 14:7).

Receiving comfort in crises and then feeling obliged to share it, is how many of our grandest hymns and literary works originated!

* "Home Sweet Home" was written by John Payne, a wanderer.

* *Pilgrim's Progress* was penned by the imprisoned John Bunyan.

* "Amazing Grace" exploded from the grateful heart of John Newton after many close brushes with death.

* "Just As I Am" came from the pen of Charlotte Elliot when she was doubting her usefulness.

* "Nearer, My God to Thee" was sent forth by Flower Adams whose poor health forced her to write.

* "What a Friend We Have in Jesus" was inspired in the heart of Joseph Scriven who wanted to encourage his mother who was ill.

When God comforts us, we are obliged to comfort others. Many times the crises of life crush us so the sweet perfume of comfort may emerge. The painter who mixes his colors with the "blood" from his own broken heart creates the best picture.

Be ready to pass on your experiences! I believe God has allowed me to go through certain family difficulties in preparation for my ministry to hurting marriages. The redeemed alcoholic discovers he stays sober by helping others with his problem. Don't run from your experiences! Patiently bear with them. Learn all you can during them . . . and you will have an opportunity to share the comfort you received with others.

2
When Conflict Comes

2 Corinthians 2:3-11

A church in the Midwest made national headlines by "withdrawing fellowship" from one of its members. Details concerning a woman charged with adultery began to surface. Church officials had met with the woman several times, urging her to dissolve a relationship deemed immoral. That church voted to dismiss the member from its membership when she refused to heed biblical counsel. In the following months, the woman in turn sued the church. Many shocked Christians watched as the application of the biblical process of reconciliation was abused and misused.

This passage before us is most instructive on how to handle offenders in the church. In every church there will be at least an occasional conflict in the church. Right? Even though the church is the body of Christ, the bride of Christ, and the family of God, it is made up of people! And people have feelings, opinions, and are at different stages of spiritual development. Unfortunately, conflict surfaces from time to time—we're not in heaven yet.

This passage of Scripture lays out definite principles about offenders and reconciliation in the church. Hopefully, we will answer the following questions:

* Could a situation arise that would warrant the expulsion of a member from a New Testament church?

* How should the congregation respond to a member who is out of fellowship?

* What would be the criteria in determining how and when to restore the member?

Have you ever been in a church where there arose a serious conflict? Many people have unpleasant memories of church conflict that was not handled correctly. Now let's look into Paul's advice in reference to church problems.

Situation

Paul wrote about something that had happened earlier in the church at Corinth. A man had caused a situation that brought grief, sorrow, and tears to Paul and the congregation (vv. 4-5). Commentators are not in agreement about the exact nature of the deed called into question by Paul. Some think Paul was referring to the situation dealt with in the first letter to the Corinthians. This flammable situation concerned a man who was committing fornication with his father's wife—a deed appalling even to lost Gentiles!

But there are other equally competent scholars who feel that the apostle had in mind another person who had rejected Paul's authority. That man was creating severe controversy in the church. So, we are not certain about the specific cause of Paul's concern in 2 Corinthians 2:3-11.

Personally, I believe Paul was pointing to the unforgettable problem in 1 Corinthians 5. For one reason, Paul did not seem to have any other specific crisis in mind. Another is that Paul had given directions to the church about how the matter should be handled (see 1 Cor. 5:4-5). It appears from consideration of this passage in 2 Corinthians 2:6 that his directions had been followed. Then, too, the highly emotional tone of the passage seems to indicate the grave situation of confronting the sin of open fornication within the church.

Churches do have problems! Satan does attack the church. Since I have been pastor of my church over fifteen years, I can identify several major frontal attacks by the enemy. Satan has aimed his poison darts at the staff, deacon body, prominent members, and the most active ministries of the church. Seldom will the devil waste time on dead members or dead programs!

A favorite attack of Satan appears to involve sexual sins. We read of movie stars, sports figures, top businessmen, and politicians who yield to temptation. Well, it is being proven that the church is not immune! The sexual revolution energized by Satan has invaded the church. In some churches, the members and even the staff have been involved in shocking adulterous affairs. I have seen and heard of sexual affairs within the sacred body of Christ that would virtually mortify Hollywood! The situation at Corinth as recorded by Paul sounds like a scandal uncovered in a tabloid paper.

Sentence

I have often talked to splendid elderly Christians about 1 Corinthians 5; 2 Corinthians 2:3-11; and Matthew 18:15-17. These are senior saints who lived before some of today's modernism, permissiveness, and secular humanism that have made a full-scale attack on the church. I have met precious few Christians who have been involved in a church where biblical discipline was exercised on one of the members!

Usually, when a member falls into open sin, one of two things happen through other church members: (1) The person is "rocked." In the Middle East during Bible days the punishment for adultery was death by stoning. Today the members hit him or her with stones of damaging criticism, censorious gossip, and condemnation. (2) The person is rejected. In Bible days the leper was ostracized, excommunicated, and rejected. Today people in sin are ignored and branded as social lepers. Seemingly, very few want to confront them in a spirit of love.

When I was a boy, one of my Sunday School teachers had a bad drinking problem. The pastor loved to go fishing with him, and, like everyone else in our little Florida town, was aware of the man's problem. One day the pastor came over to go fishing. While the man was getting the boat ready, the pastor commented to the man's wife, "I won't let on like I know anything's wrong." Years later, this man's wife confided in me, "Oh, if only the pastor had confronted my husband. We agonized through years of personal and marital hell because no one knew how to confront and help my husband!"

Do you remember Paul's suggested approach about the problem of open, flagrant sin in Corinth? Read again carefully and prayerfully 1 Corinthians 5. Could there ever be a situation that warrants expulsion from the fellowship of the church? Yes! Paul obviously felt the man had been dealt with sufficiently and had been given time to repent. Notice that the apostle puts the authority on the local church under the leadership of Jesus Christ (1 Cor. 5:4-5). This sentence is not a personal vendetta by the church leadership: it is the will of Christ through the agency of the local church.

Notice the actual sentence of the church in 1 Corinthians 5:5. The person involved is to be delivered "unto

Satan for the destruction of the flesh." What does that mean? Is that some sort of biblical voodoo where a curse is put upon a person?

Let me explain how I envision that sentence: as a child of God I am under my Father's protection and provision. Satan is a devourer, and God actually rebukes him (the devil) when he tries to steal my belongings and even my life (Mal. 3:11). We are able to grasp this from Job's experience of Satan's power. Satan has a certain ability to attack and ravage the believer. From the Bible we are also aware that God can give Satan authority to tear up one's possessions and person yet stop short of taking his or her life (Job. 2:6).

When the church at Corinth delivered the offender to Satan, they were withdrawing God's protection over that person. They prayed for whatever it would take to bring that person into submission and into God's will. By the offender's chosen life-style of disobedience and rebellion, he was forcing God to withdraw protection over him.

This is in keeping with Jesus' words concerning handling an offense as found in Matthew 18:15-17. Do you remember the steps in dealing with an offender?

1. The first step is between brother and brother (Matt. 18:15). Hopefully, two people can talk through a problem under the Lord's leadership and be reconciled. This is the how all our problems should be handled—one on one! Unfortunately, that is not the usual course of action today, as people gossip and recruit others to their side. Then there is great division within the church.

2. If the individual people cannot handle the problem satisfactorily, step two states that the matter should be discussed with witnesses present. Again, an effort is made

to restrict the knowledge of the conflict. I have been a witness in more than one confrontation and have seen harmony restored on several occasions. The witnesses are respected by both parties and can be objective and confidential.

3. The third step is to go before the church if the situation cannot be resolved through the counsel of witnesses (Matt. 18:17). Do bear in mind that the intended goal throughout this biblical process is reconciliation and restoration. At this point, if the person will not respond, then he is likened to one—an infidel, an unbeliever—outside of Christ. The church is commanded to break off fellowship and association with him. He is to be presented with the gospel again as though he were an unbeliever. It is hoped that the withdrawal of fellowship would stimulate any life of God within the sinner and drive him to confess and forsake his sin.

Please notice again in Matthew 18:15-17 the authority of the local church. A member surrenders her rights to the body of Christ. She is submissive to the authority of Christ and the church. A congregation's authority is derived from the presence of Jesus in their midst (Matt. 18:20).

The body of Christ must be protected from the infiltration and influence of sin. Remember how quickly Joshua dealt with Achan's sin in Joshua 7:16-26? And who can forget the drastic results following the sin of Ananias and Sapphira within the early church? (Acts 5). That is why Paul is so protective of the body of Christ! "Purge out therefore the old leaven, . . . [Do not keep] company with fornicators: . . . put away from among yourselves that wicked person" (1 Cor. 5:7,9,13). The sentence is intended to protect the body of Christ and take strong measures to restore the offender.

Support

The Scriptures indicate that the Corinthian church obeyed the instructions in handling the offender. The combination of firm love, obedient discipline, and energizing by God's Spirit produced a wonderfully changed heart in the one who had committed a grievous sin. This is indicated in 2 Corinthians 2:6: "Sufficient to such a man is this punishment." We praise God in seeing God's Word proven once again and a person reclaimed for productive service.

If a church exercises discipline according to God's Word and the offending person expresses a repentant spirit, what are the criteria for restoring him or her back to fellowship? I would like to mention two considerations:

1. Testimony—The person should be interviewed and counseled by the pastor and church leaders. There should be genuine admission of guilt and a contrite confession of the sin. From the offender's own mouth there should be a recognition of wrong and a desire to again be a part of God's fellowship.

2. Time—There should be a sufficient amount of time allowed for the repentant offender to indicate sincerity and stability. If there has been an adulterous affair, the church would want to see the person happily back with his own spouse (in the case of sexual sins not involving married persons, a proving time is also indicated). A period of six months to a year can be put on each situation, but there should be enough time to indicate the person has allowed the Lord to straighten out his life.

The restoration of the offender to the fellowship of the church seemingly had two parts. First of all, there were *personal actions*. Paul writes in verse 7 that the individual members should "forgive . . . and comfort him." There should be an approach by the membership to the offender to show love and tenderness. He should be buoyed by personal exhortations and assurances of Christian consolation. No doubt there were many within the church body who had been personally hurt by the offender's actions or who had taken offense on behalf of the offender's spouse. These would have to settle any anger or bitterness in their own hearts before they could demonstrate genuine forgiveness.

A young woman in our church became pregnant out of wedlock. In a touching, emotion-charged service, her father, mother, and the young woman made a confession before our church. When they had completed their heart-rending confessions, I said, "Now you've heard their confessions. We can either "rock" them, reject them, or restore them. What will it be?" One by one, our people came out of the pews to hug and encourage this family. What a glorious sight! Paul said, "Forgive . . . and comfort him."

A second part of the process, however, involved *public action*. In verse 8 we find the words: "Wherefore I beseech you that ye would confirm your love toward him." The word *confirm* is a legal word. It literally means to ratify an agreement, such as a will. Paul is saying that the church had taken public action to discipline and withdraw fellowship. Now the church should take public action to ratify their forgiveness and restoration. Again, we emphasize the authority of the local church body. Paul said in 1 Corinthians 5:4: "In the name of our Lord Jesus Christ, when ye are gathered together." I emphasize the phrase "gathered together" because that indicates the church made the decision to withdraw fellowship. Now they gather together again to restore that fellowship. The vote to confirm the individual would indicate love and forgiveness and admission back into full fellowship of the body.

It was as important for the church to forgive, comfort, and confirm the offender as it was for the offender to admit wrong and confess. Paul gave a great insight into why the church must forgive and affirm forgiveness: "Lest perhaps such a one should be swallowed up with overmuch sorrow" (2 Cor. 2:7). Imagine the broken heart of one who feels she may never be forgiven and accepted! The picture of sorrow filling one's heart to the brim, and then running over, is most vivid in verse 7. Forgiveness graciously empties that broken heart filled with sorrow.

Once two men had kept an unsettled feud for years. Hard bitterness was between them, and it had poisoned both of their respective families. One of the men was about to die, and he called for the other man. "I'm not long for this earth," the old man began. "And I just wanted to get everything settled before I crossed over. Will your forgive me?" The old man's longtime adversary eyed his enemy who was just a shell of the man he once had been. "Yes, I forgive you," he said. They shook hands and were about to part when the dying man roused himself and proclaimed, "Now, if I come through all of this, you know it's back like it used to be between us!"

Satan uses the spirit of unforgiveness to his satanic glory. All of us have seen the effects of hurt turning into bitterness when people do not forgive.

The thrill of the story lies in the fact that the Corinthian prodigal son came home! His heart was made right, and he recognized the need of his spiritual family. The father (represented by the Corinthian church) forgave and accepted the wayward member. Support was given personally and publicly.

Suggestions

Now let me make two suggestions about handling church conflict:

1. *Understand the Infection of Sin*—Before a man left home, he alibied to his son: "Son, my life is my own. I'm not going to hurt anyone else. I'm going to do what is best for me." The father did not realize how much his action would affect and infect the futures of his two children. What you do influences others just as the stone thrown into the water produces far-reaching ripples. An alcoholic cannot isolate his problem but infects fifteen to twenty-five other people.

When we, as Christians, fall into sin, we are not isolated with the effects of our sin. We infect others and, especially, heap reproach on the body of Christ. Do you see what ramifications this has concerning confession? We confess the sin as far as the sin is known! If it is between us and God, it is *private* confession. If it is between us and someone else, it becomes *personal* confession between the involved parties. And, if it is known by the church, then it becomes *public* confession before the body of Christ. Let us understand the infection of sin.

2. *Understand the Influence of Sin*—Jesus explained that "if ye do not forgive, neither will your Father which is in heaven forgive your trespasses" (Mark 11:26). If people harbor the sin of unforgiveness in their hearts, they cannot expect forgiveness from God. May I say it in another way: until people are forgiven by God, they cannot forgive others! This is a disastrous influence of sin.

The Jews are God's people, but they need to be forgiven. The world watches as the Israeli war-criminal hunters track down another German. There is another spectacular, vengeful trial. Usually the prisoner is guilty of horrible crimes committed against the Jewish people and sentenced to death or life imprisonment. What do you think would happen if the Jewish people would make this national statement: "We know this man is guilty, but we forgive him of his crimes"? What a shock! But more than likely that will never happen. Only people forgiven by God have the deepest capacity to forgive others. No one, not even God's "chosen people," can properly forgive until they have embraced the Messiah who cried from the cross, "Father, forgive them, for they know not what they do."

As a pastor, I see this principle illustrated in many ways. Perhaps the most prevalent application lies in the area of divorce. Usually there are so many hurt and bitter feelings surrounding a divorce. Also, there are few people who confess divorce as a sin and receive forgiveness. Only then can they forgive the offending spouse and relatives. That is why pastors view such messy situations surrounding the breakup of marriages: the ones confessing their sins are forgiven and are now capable of forgiving others. They are now part of the solution and not part of the problem.

As a member of the church, are you part of the solution or the problem? Do you have a forgiving spirit because you have been forgiven by God? Is there an outcast member to whom you should go and forgive, comfort, and confirm? "For to this end also did I write, that I might know the proof of you, whether ye be obedient in all things" (2 Cor. 2:9).

3
The Gospel Fragrance

2 Corinthians 2:14-16

A famous Hollywood actress announced the creation of her own personal perfume. A tour of America's major cities followed where the actress and the perfume were honored at vast gatherings of the rich and famous. The newspapers reported that the scent of "Passion" had been left across America through the marketing of this actress's perfume.

Millions of dollars are spent each year to enhance the fragrance of people around the world. Colognes, perfumes, powders, and a pervasive array of fragrances receive attention through television and media. Sports stars help us "smell like a man" while beautiful actresses encourage us to use expensive perfumes to be alluring and seductive.

Recently, a new perfume was introduced that is of interest to Bible students. Oman Perfumery's "Amouage" perfume is based on the ingredients of frankincense and myrrh. This perfume will sell for about $375 an ounce, making it the world's most expensive perfume. Those who have tried it say that it is "myrrhvelous!"

Each of us can associate various memories of happenings in life with specific odors. The smell of the operating room, with its anesthetics and medicines, is unforgettable. Men would certainly remember the smell of the grass during summer football practices. Male and female alike enjoy the delightful smells of the newborn baby's bedroom. Various perfumes or colognes carry adults back to their teen dating days. The sense of smell certainly is a vital part of our lives.

Did you know that there is a gospel odor? Would you be amazed to hear that a Christian has a specific fragrance? You have heard preaching about your walk and talk, but when was the last time you were asked how you smelled? Here is a vivid section to the Corinthians concerning the fragrance of the gospel.

Processional Fragrance

No doubt the Roman Empire was one of the greatest powers in the history of humankind. No other empire controlled such vast territories with so few men. At its zenith, the Roman Empire of more than fifty million people was protected by an army of only three hundred thousand soldiers. Superior organization, dedication, and discipline characterized the magnificent Roman army.

The Roman Triumph is described in this passage. Few events in the lifetime of the Roman citizen were as thrilling as the Roman Triumph. After a resounding military campaign where a victory was won on foreign soil, the conquering general was treated to a thrilling procession into Rome. Only if the general had won a complete victory over the enemy, where at least five thousand were killed and new territory was seized for Rome, could he be entitled to a Triumph. This would be equivalent to the famous ticker tape-parade awarded to an American's outstanding achievement.

The Roman army would enter the city in a prescribed order. At the front of the procession would come the leaders of the state and senate. Following them would be the captives of the conquered nation who would be freed and made Roman citizens. Booty, spoil, and conquered treasure would be displayed in the next section of the procession. Then would appear the white bull which would be offered as a sacrifice. The captured army would come next, wretched captives dragged in chains behind chariots or displayed in cages. Musicians would come heralding the honored general. The center of the parade featured the conquering general riding in a opulent gold chariot drawn by four horses. The general would be attired in royal purple with an ivory scepter in his hand and a victor's garland on his head. After the general came his family and then the entire Roman army. It was a moving sight!

The Roman Triumph entered the city in a prescribed route. Resembling New Orleans's Mardi Gras, the procession would wind its way through the noted streets of Rome. One stop would be at the national temple where sacrifices would be offered to Jupiter. Another visit would be at the Circus Maximus where conquered captives would either be killed by the wild beasts or publicly executed. The final destination would be at the emperor's palace where devotion would be expressed by the general and army to the nation's leader. The emperor would pronounce a public honor on the conquering general and his army. Pride and thanksgiving would be expressed by the emperor.

The sights and sounds of the Roman Triumph were thrilling. But there was another impressive dimension to that monumental day: the smells. Resembling the famous Rose Bowl Parade, the Roman Triumph was full of delicious, delirious fragrances. Flowers in abundance were

strewn along the route and thrown to the victorious soldiers. Roman priests carried bowls of scented, smoking incense during the entire parade. The smoke of incense
sometimes would obscure the sight of the parade.

There is a renewed interest today in various types of
incense burning. It is not unusual to enter homes where
leaves or bark are being heated on the stove or warmed
beneath candles. The house has a delightful fragrance
that blesses both guest and host.

Captors and captives alike would smell the incense
along the entire Roman procession. The whole city would
be under the influence of the incense of the Roman
priests. It was a once-in-a-lifetime event, and the smells of
the day would long be remembered. It is important that
we perceive Paul's description of processional fragrance.

Personal Fragrance

Did you know that each person has his/her own "spiritual odor"? We are all either "dead in trespasses and
sins" (Eph. 2:1) or "quickened" and made alive (Eph. 2:1).
If we are not alive unto God, then our unregenerated nature surely must have the spiritual smell of death to it.
Without Christ "we are all as an unclean thing, and all
our righteousnesses are as filthy rags" (Isa. 64:6). These
rags are compared to leper's bandages, and they surely
smell like death. Death has a foul-smelling odor and can
be likened to the spiritual state of an unbeliever.

The child of God has the unmistakable spiritual odor of
life upon him. This is made possible because of Jesus' re-
demptive work which overcomes the effects of death.
Christ "hath given himself for us an offering and a sacrifice to God for a sweet-smelling savor" (Eph. 5:2). Jesus'
death on the cross was accepted by God as payment for
our sins. By receiving Jesus as Savior and Lord, "we are

unto God a sweet savor of Christ" (2 Cor. 2:15). So, how do you smell spiritually? Do you know Jesus Christ? If so, you can shout with Paul: "Thanks be unto God, which always causeth us to triumph in Christ, and maketh manifest the savor of his knowledge by us in every place" (2 Cor. 2:14). We smell good or acceptable to God through His Son, Jesus Christ.

There is an old saying that goes about like this: "They came out of that smelling like a rose." Paul wants us to know that in Christ we are always on the victorious side, and we will always be smelling good.

An unforgettable illustration of this concerns the three Hebrews in Nebuchadnezzar's fiery furnace. Remember how these three were being punished for refusing to bow down to the image of a man rather than to God. The punishment was death by burning in a specially prepared furnace. How thrilling to recall that God Himself was with them in the fiery furnace (Dan. 3:25). The fire had no power on them and, when the three were removed from the furnace, it was noted: "Nor was an hair of their head singed, neither were their coats changed, nor the smell of fire had passed on them" (Dan. 3:27). The faithful believers came out of the battle smelling good! They were on the winning side which always triumphs!

What would be considered your personal fragrance? A smell of life in Christ or the smell of death without Christ? From God's vantage point, we do not possess the proper spiritual fragrance until Christ is in us.

Providential Fragrance

There is a final, dramatic point concerning the fragrance accompanying the Roman Triumph. We remember that the entire procession would be enveloped by the odor of the incense. The conquering general and the victorious Romans would smell the incense, and this would be the fragrance of joy, victory, and life. But, to the conquered captives who faced public torture and death at the end of the march, the incense became the fragrance of death. It was the same smell, but it meant different things to different people in the procession.

Receiving different impressions from the same fragrance can be illustrated in several ways. An athlete's dressing room is full of the smells of liniment, tape, and dirty clothes. To the athlete this is home and heaven, but it would be repulsive to many people, both men and women. There are areas of large department stores, namely the cosmetics counters, where women love to congregate. But you will find mostly men there only on Valentine's Day and other gift occasions! The nursery at our church smells so good with the fragrances of powder and babies. Most people love to go there, but how do you think this sets with the couple who has lost a baby or who cannot have one? There can be smells of life and smells of death.

Along the procession of the Roman Triumph were two classes of people among whom this perfume circulated. To the victors, the perfume was a symbol of present gladness and future safety. To the captives, the aroma became a token of defeat, condemnation, and approaching death.

With that disturbing scenario in mind, Paul said that each one possessing Jesus Christ becomes the gospel fragrance. Each minister and disciple is a vessel or dispenser of the gospel fragrance. To God, the believer is the very fragrance of Jesus Christ, His Son. To other believers, the believer is the fragrance of life. To unbelievers, the believer is the fragrance of death. The way we live and work can mean life or death to a lost world around us. We are incense giving forth the fragrance of Jesus in our lives and labors.

What kind of fragrance or influence are you dispensing each day? A lady climbed aboard a city bus one day. She complained about everything from the moment she arrived. Everyone around her was subjected to a barrage of griping, complaining, and bitter words. As the lady climbed down the stairs to leave the bus, the driver said, "Lady, you left something." She felt for her purse and umbrella and looked back at the seat she had just vacated.

"What did I leave?" she asked.

"You left a bad impression," asserted the bus driver. When we leave a room or a home, do we leave a sweet fragrance or influence of the gospel?

Paul viewed himself and all other believers as being conquered by Christ. In reality, everyone is a part of the Gospel Triumph procession. People are either on the victorious gospel side or the defeated unbeliever side. Paul often referred to himself as a prisoner of the Lord, and he did it with joy. The difference now is that we are God's trophies and not His enemies. We were not conquered by the sword but by the love of the cross. We now joyfully march in His triumphant team. Our constant cry along the Gospel Triumph procession is: "Thanks be unto God, which always causeth us to triumph in Christ" (2 Cor. 2:14).

Spiritually speaking, we carry the gospel fragrance or the "savor of his knowledge by us in every place" (2 Cor. 2:14). May your life and mine be so lived that we are a fragrance of life unto life.

4
When Satan Goes to Church

2 Corinthians 2:11; 4:4; 11:14

Do you believe in the existence of a real-life Satan? Surveys indicate that more people believe in heaven than in hell. A survey was taken at an "ecumenical council" where 521 clergy and laity were asked about Jesus and the devil. Results showed that little more than 50 percent believed Jesus to be divine. One third of those polled declared that the devil definitely does not exist!

The apostle Paul believed in Satan. Out of thirteen chapters in 2 Corinthians, Satan's influence is mentioned in four of them (2:11; 4:4; 11:3,14; 12:7).

During World War II, a group of soldiers crowded around their chaplain as the ship crossed the ocean en route of their theater of operations. They asked the chaplain, "Do you believe in hell?"

The chaplain replied that he did not believe in hell. "Well, sir, will you please resign?" the soldiers implored. "For if there is no hell, we don't need you. And, if there is a hell, we do not wish to be led astray!"

As you study the Bible, you cannot help noticing the activity of Satan. This chapter will attempt to summarize and classify his work in Corinth. I will begin by calling attention to Paul's *description of Satan,* then will examine the startling *deception of Satan,* and finally *the devices of Satan.* Please concentrate! Satan is a master at distraction.

Why don't people respond to the good news of the gospel? As lost as humans are without Christ, you would think they would actually run after the gospel! Paul makes it plain in 2 Corinthians 4:4 that people remain lost because of the activity of Satan. Satan blinds the eyes of humankind, so the light of the gospel cannot shine into their hearts. Paul further described Satan as the "god of this world" (v. 4).

Who can deny the existence of a mastermind of evil? There must be a hidden author of sin plotting the awful things happening to the world! Gideons International is stationed in Donelson, Tennessee, not far from our church. One of my favorite rooms in the Gideons building is the "War Room." Usually, this room has an enlarged map of a major city all around the walls. The Gideons have marked every school, hospital, motel, and hotel in that city. Each one is targeted to have Gideons converge on that cite to distribute the Word of God.

It is not difficult for me to visualize Satan's "War Room" with the continents of the world broken down into countries, states, cities, and people. Plans are made by this mastermind to wage war on every person on earth in order that he or she does not receive Jesus Christ.

Look at these evidences of war by this author of evil:

* The downward trend of society throwing off every restraint.

* The divorce and heartbreaking condition of the home and family. Divorce is approaching 50 percent of all marriages.

* There are ten to twelve million alcoholics (whom society is aware of), and their ranks are growing at the rate of 1500 per day.

* The unbelievable power of the drug culture.

* There are at least one million runaway children each year, and this does not include the throwaway children or the escalation of child abuse.

* Almost one million teenage girls will become pregnant out of wedlock each year. Satan will persuade 400,000 of them to kill their babies through abortion.

* People are asserting their "rights" as never before! We have demonstrations by prisoners, students, and gays.

* There is unparalleled occurrence of crime and violence in our world: a true spirit of lawlessness. Last year we had over 70,000 public school teachers assaulted.

* Wars all over the world.

* The prevailing philosophy of humanism in our land. There is permissiveness in our homes, schools, and prisons.

* We have a generation of parents who do not know their own children. Many of those who know their children are afraid of them.

* We have a generation of preachers who do not preach the doctrines of sin, hell, and salvation truthfully and forcefully.

* We have a generation of Christians who are afraid to share Jesus. The soul-winner is becoming extinct. One expert estimates 95 percent of Christians in the church have never led a soul to Christ. Satan has convinced the Christian to love the world more than God.

* We have a generation of people who do not know right from wrong. People do what is right in their own eyes.

I submit to you that the author of this heinous list of crimes against humanity is Satan. Only the Bible dares to describe him. Notice some of the other descriptions of our enemy, the devil:

* First Peter 5:8 calls him our "adversary." He opposes us.

* First Peter 5:8 further reveals him as a "roaring lion, who walketh about, seeking whom he may devour." The devil is not a lovable pussycat—as he would lead people to believe—but a roaring lion!

* First Thessalonians 3:5 labels him as a "tempter" or one who seduces.

* John 8:44 says that Satan is a "murderer" and "a liar." This description comes from the lips of our Lord Himself. When we call someone a murderer and a liar, we had better have our facts straight. Jesus spoke the shocking truth about Satan.

* Ephesians 2:2 calls Satan the "prince and power of the air."

* Revelation 12:10 describes Satan as "the accuser of our brethren."

From the above evidence, we believe Satan is not just an impersonal power or force. He is a person. His success depends on being anonymous—only the Bible dares to expose him.

In 2 Corinthians 4:4 Satan is called the "god of this world." It is admitted that he has power, a kingdom, and is worshiped. People bow before him and follow him. Look at all the different areas of life today. Wherever the truth of Jesus isn't followed, Satan rules! Examine the worlds of business, pleasure, and fashions: Does Jesus rule there, or does Satan?

Remember when Jesus was tempted? In one temptation Jesus was shown all the kingdoms of the world. Satan said: "All these things I will give thee, if thou wilt fall
down and worship me" (Matt. 4:9). Satan implied that the
kingdoms of the world were under his rule. That is what
Paul meant when he called Satan the "god of this world."
That is Satan's description.

Deception of Satan

We have seen the true nature and character of Satan.
He is called an adversary, an accuser, a deceiver, a liar, a
lion, a murderer, a tempter, and the god of this world. A
logical question might be: "If this is the way Satan is, how
does he persuade people to follow and serve him?"

Another profound mention of Satan in 2 Corinthians
occurs in 11:14. Paul further exposes the enemy: "No
marvel; for Satan himself is transformed as an angel of
light." Paul had been talking about false prophets who
had deceived the fellowship of believers: How could anyone believe such liars? Because, as Paul pointed out, they
act in a masquerade and put on a disguise. They pretend
to be something they are not. The apostle emphasized
that these false teachers are imitating their satanic
master as they transform themselves into "ministers of
righteousness" (v. 15).

After seeing Satan's true description, one wonders how
he persuades innocent souls to follow him into sin, degra-
dation, and destruction. The answer is that Satan is able
to drape a disguise over his nature of darkness and become an "angel of light." In 2 Corinthians 11:14, the Bible
says Satan is "transformed." "Transform" means to disguise, to masquerade, and to hide behind a mask. This awful beast of evil never appears in true character. He is

always in disguise. He has an ability to conceal an assumed virtue behind a facade. He is the creature capable of thousands of disguises!

Satan realizes people will not accept the ugly truth about him. So he baits his hook with deceit. He makes evil appear desirable. In the end, the devil is able to convince people that his offer is better than God's!

Think about Achan. Achan (Josh. 7) was with the Israelites when they attacked Jericho. We remember God's specific instructions for Israel to avoid contact with any gold, silver, or treasure of Jericho. These were to go into God's treasury (Josh. 6:18-19). The person who kept them would be accursed. The sad truth was that Achan kept for himself some gold, silver, and Babylonian clothing. His explanation for his sin was: "I saw . . . I coveted them, and took them" (Josh. 7:21).

This confession was punctuated with the influence of Satan! A crafty charlatan, Satan induced Achan to disregard God's clear command. The hook Satan baited with gold, silver, and Babylonian clothing was more appealing than obedience to Almighty God. Achan obviously ignored the awful consequences to himself, his family, and his nation.

I have seen men sell their souls because of greed and lust. A man looks at the sacred money of his business and envisions a possible new house or vacation, so he embezzles. Another man is having problems at home. Satan provides attractive bait in the form of a woman at work, so adultery is the result. In both cases, the men were convinced by Satan that the sin would be better for them than being obedient to God. In both cases, the men never considered the far-reaching consequences to themselves, their families, or the cause of Christ. Satan is deceptive!

Today literally thousands of people claim to be Satan

worshipers. Many of these are hardened, sinful people whose consciences are seemingly beyond the power of the gospel. How did they become like this? All at once? No, studies indicate Satan worshipers begin with the simple attraction of astrology and horoscopes. One in five Americans expresses belief in astrology. Occult and so-called "New Age" books, tapes, and paraphernalia sales have doubled in the last four years. Satan has baited his hook with the seemingly harmless practice of observing the daily horoscopes. This practice opens the person to further satanic exercises and eventually to witchcraft. Satan is a deceiver!

Consider the sins of alcohol or drug addiction. Do you think Satan would show you the true results of drinking alcoholic beverages: cirrhosis of the liver, job losses, broken homes, traffic fatalities, or even "crimes of passion" like violent murder of a spouse or a child? Would he paint the true picture of the drug user in a stupor or ODing himself to death. That is not how the master deceiver will "hook" you. He will exhibit on television some of the greatest athletes in the world advertising beer. People will think: *If this outstanding athlete can drink and achieve such attainments in sports, then drinking must be all right.* Oh, what a dirty deceiver Satan is!

Devices of Satan

Satan has two main goals. One is to keep people from being saved. The second goal is (if he loses someone to Jesus) to neutralize the effectiveness of Christians.

Paul states in 2 Corinthians 2:11 that Satan has devices: "Lest Satan should get an advantage of us: for we are not ignorant of his devices." The word *devices* refers to schemes, plots, strategies, or evil plans and purposes.

Satan plots. He plans. He maps out strategies for opposing the gospel.

When Paul first mentioned Satan's devices, he was referring to the local situation at Corinth. Talk about an evil plan! Satan devised a complicated scheme in Corinth: first, he lured an individual member to commit fornication with his father's wife. Paul countered this by giving wise counsel on how to deal with sin in the church. When the church acted, Satan plotted a spirit of unforgiveness in the church and a spirit of discouragement in the individual offender. If Satan had achieved his goal, he would have accomplished the following: turned a man away from God, split a church, discredited the apostle Paul, and spread an evil report to the pagan world about the failure of Christ's church. What a scheme!

One of the Christian's defenses against Satan's devices is a prior awareness of his purposes and methods. To the Bible-based Christian, Satan is very predictable. Also bear in mind that he is still more powerful than we are without Christ. But I believe his devices can be categorized into three general areas:

Doubt—All of us *are* familiar with the tempter's subterfuge to Eve in the Garden of Eden: "Hath God said? . . ." (Gen. 3:1). When faced with temptation, haven't you heard Satan's whisper about the real truth of God's Word. "Does God really mean what He says?" "God doesn't want you to have any fun." "That Book is so outdated and old-fashioned—it doesn't apply to today!" Satan will endeavor to make you doubt God's Word.

Let's use Achan again for an example. Achan heard God's clear command against keeping accursed articles from Jericho. Satan whispered in Achan's ear: "You don't believe God would kill you for claiming something you deserve after a hard battle, do you? You, one of God's chosen people?" That little doubt soon turned into disrespect for God's command. Then a total disregard dominated with the end result of blatant disobedience. Satan had claimed another victim. It all began with a doubt of God's Word.

Divide—The second great device of Satan is division. We remember Jesus said: "Every kingdom divided against itself is brought to desolation; and every city or house divided against itself shall not stand" (Matt. 12:25). How Satan loves to divide churches! Much of the New Testament is written to counteract the strategy of Satan's divisions. Cliques, abuse of spiritual gifts, ignorance of the woman's role, open sin, and the abuse of the Lord's Supper were some of the devices at Corinth used to divide the church. Remember, "God is not the author of confusion, but of peace, as in all churches of the saints" (1 Cor. 14:33).

Satan loves to divide the family. Every marital unrest, separation, or divorce was caused by Satan's division. Satan absolutely hates a happy, Christlike home. Why? Because it is a picture of heaven on earth. He aims his most powerful darts at our homes in an effort to split them. Today almost 50 percent of all marriages end in divorce. Over 50 percent of the children under five are being raised in single parent homes. There are more than 2,000,000 unrelated people living together out of wedlock. Children run away from home. Parents are forsaking their responsibilities of the home. Satan is a great divider!

Delay—I suspect that the number-one reason for people ending up with Satan in hell will be "delay." Most people, deep within their hearts, know there is a God. These same people realize that this life is not the end. Within all of our hearts we have the feeling that there will be a great reckoning some day. Why, then, do people die lost? The main reason is that Satan persuades them to keep postponing their commitment to Jesus Christ. We know:

* John 1:12 says we must receive Christ.

* Romans 10:13 says we must "call upon the name of the Lord."

* Revelation 3:20 says that we must "open the door."

God works in us, reproving us of sin, righteousness, and judgment (John 16:8). The faith we need to believe is given to us by God (Eph. 2:8). God does all things necessary to prepare us for salvation, but there comes that time when we must receive, call on the Lord's name, and open the door. When it comes to that time of personal commitment, Satan will give us some excuse to put off, to procrastinate, and to postpone that important decision.

A great revival was sweeping Princeton University many years ago. A concerned student went to the president. "I have made up my mind to consider the claims of Christ. What would you do?" The president thought for a moment and then replied, "If I were you, I'd wait until the excitement of the revival has subsided. Then I would think it out carefully." The student, Aaron Burr, followed the president's advice. People who knew Burr said he never again expressed a desire to become a Christian. If the devil can, he will cause each of us to delay.

Satan! Are you now aware of his description? He will never appear as he actually is, but he will play the game of deception. Are you now aware of his devices aimed at ushering in doubt, division, and delay into our lives. "Be sober, be vigilant; because your adversary the devil, as a roaring lion, walketh about, seeking whom he may devour: Whom resist steadfast in the faith" (1 Pet. 5:8-9).

5
The Inward Man

2 Corinthians 4:16-18

The legal world of America received a shock when a brilliant judge committed suicide. His peers ranked this man as one of the greatest judges in the history of the federal bench. A fellow judge said: "There was nothing that he did not do well." Following the death, investigators found several notes which mentioned his heavy grief over his wife's passing. They had been married for fifty-five years. A good friend commented: "Her death was quite a blow to him. They had been very, very close. He simply lost his will to live after she died."

The apostle Paul gives a message to us in 2 Corinthians 4:16 that applies to the above true story: "For which cause we faint not." The word *faint* means to lose courage, to lose heart, to give up or give in, and to behave badly. Paul defies any situation that could cause a child of God to faint.

And, yet, all around us we see people losing heart and giving in to outside pressures:

* Each suicide means a person lost heart and gave up on life.

* The staggering number of marriage breakups mean people could not hold onto their commitments.

* Burnout has attacked in epidemic proportions. Pressures in life cause people to faint.

* Our churches are beset with absenteeism and apostasy. On practically any given Sunday, less than half of a church's membership will be present. People lose heart at the slightest provocation and leave the church. The body of Christ is hindered dramatically by spiritual dropouts.

Does the child of God ever faint? Notice these revealing passages on the subject of fainting:

* "Let us not be weary in well-doing: for in due season we shall reap, if we faint not" (Gal. 6:9).

* "I would not have you to be ignorant, brethren, concerning them which are asleep, that ye sorrow not, even as others which have no hope" (1 Thess. 4:13).

* "Therefore, my beloved brethren, be ye steadfast, unmovable, always abounding in the work of the Lord, forasmuch as ye know that your labor is not in vain in the Lord" (1 Cor. 15:58).

The child of God, then, does not faint or sorrow as the unsaved people of the world. From these passages an important principle emerges that forms a spiritual motif for this message: *when outside pressures become stronger than inside resources, then we faint.* We are in a dangerous position when our fears and worries on the outside are greater than our faith and hope on the inside. Remember Jesus said: "Men ought always to pray, and not to faint" (Luke 18:1).

Four premises are presented in 2 Corinthians 4:16-18 to encourage us to develop our inward person to face outside pressures. Our spiritual goal is to reach the place in Christ where it may be said: "For which cause we faint not."

Duality of Natures

Before Paul instructs us concerning spiritual development, he lays a foundation with the subject of people's

dual natures. Notice the terms Paul uses in verse 16—
"outward man" and "inward man." These terms are not
to be confused with Paul's later designations, "old man"
and "new man," in Colossians 3:8-14. The "old" and
"new" descriptions of humans refer to their unregener-
ate and regenerate natures.

Precious spiritual truths become vivid to us as we realize we do indeed possess an "outward" and an "inward"
person.

1. *Outward* refers to our body. When Paul used the
term "outward,"he was referring to the physical nature
of a person. Three basic needs are met by the "outward
man" or woman.

A. *Vitality*—Through the physical body we relate to
the physical world around us. We have the five senses of
touch, taste, sight, smell, and sound. Through these
senses we are able to live comfortably and happily in
God's physical world.

B. *Visibility*—Through the physical body we are able
to have an identity in the world. The genetic makeup God
gives to us through our unique physical combinations en-
ables us to be recognized as persons.

C. *Vehicle*—Through the physical body we are able to
live our lives on earth as "souls." The real us is carried
about in our physical bodies. Our bodies, then, are instruments or carriers of the "inward" self. Just as God inhab-
ited the Old Testament tabernacle, our spiritual natures
tabernacle a brief time in our physical bodies. Just as
Jesus lived in a human body while on earth for His re-
demptive mission, our "inward" self uses the vehicle of
the "outward" self to live on earth.

Earlier in the chapter Paul used a beautiful description
to illustrate the duality of human nature. Verse 7 says:
"We have this treasure in earthen vessels." Our bodies

are the "earthen vessels" and, as such, possess the same elements as the dirt and earth. Because these bodies are made from the earth, one day they will decompose and return to the earth. Until then, the body exists for no independent purpose other than to house the soul.

2. *The Inward Self* refers to the real person in the body. We could say the inward self is the person in the man or woman. There are two parts of the inward self:

A. *Soul*—A human is a "living soul" (Gen. 2:7). This term describes the total personality but could be broken down into three distinct parts: (1) the Mind: thinking and reasoning processes; (2) the Will: volition and decision processes; and (3) the Emotions: feelings. Combine all three, and we have the actual life that energizes the lump of clay called a body.

B. *Spirit*—Before Adam's fall, the man and woman walked in perfect fellowship with God. As the highest of God's creation, human beings were created in God's image (Gen. 1:27). Since Adam's sin, each person has been "dead in trespasses and sins" and has required the miracle of a spiritual quickening to know God (Eph. 2:1,5). Through the spirit, human beings possess the ability to know and relate to God. "The Spirit itself beareth witness with our spirit, that we are the children of God" (Rom. 8:16).

This duality of human nature might be illustrated by a tree. The "outward" self corresponds to the bark, limbs, and leaves. The sap and inner life of the tree would form the "inward" self.

In like manner, Paul says we have an "outward" self which houses our soul and spirit and through which we relate to the physical world. Also, we have an "inward" self through which we relate to God and the spiritual world.

Paul proceeded to explain how a human's two natures are affected by the processes of life.

The Decline of the Outward Man

The "outward" self is described as perishing. *Perish* means to corrupt, decay, and waste away. Our physical bodies are wearing out as we grow older. Life has a way of taking its toll on us physically. Isaiah said it this way: "We all do fade as a leaf" (Isa. 64:6).

Paul probably felt the aging process working on him as he penned these words. He had traveled many miles on foot for the Lord. He had suffered hunger and cold on many occasions. The trauma of a shipwreck never left him. Prisons had become his hosts in many cities. Three times the expert of the lash had laid thirty-nine stripes across his back. Yes, Paul could feel his outward man declining.

The most vivid portrait of the outward self's decline is found in Ecclesiastes 12:3-6. Note how the body perishes:

* The "keepers of the house shall tremble"—shaky hands
* "The strong men shall bow themselves"—weakened legs
* "The grinders cease because they are few"—losing teeth
* "Those that look out of the windows be darkened"—eyes become weak with glaucoma or cataracts
* "Doors shall be shut in the streets"—mouth closed by stroke, coma
* "Sound of the grinding is low"—ears become deaf
* "Rise up at the voice of the bird" - unable to sleep
* "Daughters of music shall be brought low"—weakened vocal cords

* "Afraid of that which is high"—fear of falls; balance, equilibrium
* "Almond tree shall flourish"—hair turns white
* "Grasshopper shall be a burden"—no strength or endurance
* "Desire shall fail"—diminished sexual appetite
* "Silver cord be loosed"—spinal column gives way
* "Golden bowl be broken"—arteries in brain hemorrhage
* "Pitcher be broken at the fountain"—heart attack

As we grow older, we will experience the perishing of our outward selves. Our physical abilities will diminish and decline.

The experiences of life produce wear and tear on one's-body. Stresses, such as the death of a loved one, divorce, or financial difficulties affect our physical nature drastically. Many experts in medicine believe cancer and other diseases have emotional disturbances as their chief cause. We are only now beginning to appreciate how stress and emotional disturbances affect our outward selves.

We have seen public officials, such as presidents, age before our eyes. The graying of the hair and wrinkling are two obvious aging characteristics we have witnessed. Yes, our outward selves perish. But there is good news!

The Development of the Inward Man

Paul made a profound statement: our inward selves are renewed as our outward selves perish. The term *renewed* means to be restored or strengthened. In other words, our spirits and souls are increasing while the powers of our bodies are decreasing.

This may sound contradictory and confusing: the decline of our physical powers actually contribute to the development and increase of our spiritual powers. We have noted earlier how the experiences of life literally attack our physical body. Paul says that, as we are attacked on the outside, we become more attached to Christ on the inside. We grow spiritually as the outside physical beatings drive us to find refuge in Jesus as the Shepherd of our souls.

The trials of life bring us closer to our Lord. The very sufferings which leave human beings with weakened bodies may be the very storms which strengthen their souls.

Once a man had the meanest dog in the world. He walked down the street with that dog on a leash, and everyone was frightened. After coming to a restaurant, the owner tied the dog outside and went inside to eat supper. Soon a little man came breathlessly to his table exclaiming, "Mister, you'd better come quick. My dog has just about killed your dog!"

The man looked up and replied, 'Your dog has about killed my dog? Why, my dog is the meanest dog around these parts. What kind of dog do you have?"

The little man answered, "A Chihuahua."

"How in the world could your little Chihuahua be about to kill my dog?"

The little man explained, "He's caught in your dog's throat!"

It is not the size of the dog in the fight that counts but the size of the fight in the dog! As the battles come, our inward selves are strengthened. We do not lose our faith; rather we learn to use it. The years which take away our physical strength should add spiritual strength to our souls. We not only hold our ground but stand and win!

Notice how Paul described the outside attacks and the inward resources in verses 8 and 9:

  * troubled on every side, yet not distressed
  * perplexed, but not in despair

   * persecuted, but not forsaken
   * cast down, but not destroyed

Yes, the fights will come. The storms will attack. These will drive us to our Bibles and to our quiet times with God. As our outward selves perish, our inward selves will be renewed day by day.

Delight in the Spiritual World

What a perspective the apostle Paul had about life! He was not disturbed as his outward body perished and pushed him closer to the grave. Instead, Paul used those trials to develop his inward man and draw closer to his blessed Lord. With a perspective like that, how would Paul view affliction?

1. *"Light"*—First of all, Paul saw affliction as "light" (v. 17). This descriptive word means light in weight or easy to bear. Paul's delight in the spiritual world was such that he surveyed the extent of affliction and called it "light." There are at least three reasons affliction can be viewed as light:

A. *Compared to What We Deserve*—Thank God we have received mercy and not justice! If, during one's life-time, he received all he deserved, how miserable his existence would be. Once my family and I were returning from vacation, and I was pulled over by the state police for speeding. Really, it was a genuine speed trap if I ever I saw one—the speed limit plummeted from 50 miles per hour to 20 within a quarter of a mile. No one could gear down that fast! The police pulled another man over immediately before me and had his tickets already written before we left our cars. It was a trap! I complained about it for several miles down the road. Finally, my wife said, "Billie, you got what you deserved. You've broken the speed limit the whole time we've been gone, and it has just caught up with you!" Our affliction is light because we never get all we deserve.

B. *Compared to What Others Have Endured*—If you ever feel you have problems, you can always look around and find someone who has more. "I was unhappy because I had no shoes. Then I saw a man who had no feet!" I have been sick, but I've never been in a hospital. My wife and I have had our share of disagreements, but we are still together. My children have disobeyed, but they've never run away from home. I have been in debt, but I have never had to declare bankruptcy.

Compared to others, our afflictions are light. It would require volumes to describe afflictions of missionaries—we have suffered little compared to them! May God forgive our complaining. Read Hebrews 11:32-40 when you feel afflicted.

C. *Compared to Future Blessings*—Paul said the afflictions were light compared to all that God has in store for us in heaven. Remember Paul's praise in 1 Corinthians 2:9? "Eye hath not seen, nor ear heard, neither have entered into the heart of man, the things which God hath prepared for them that love Him." The blessings will be worth the buffetings! The glory will be worth the gloom!

We remember that Jesus endured the cross and despised the shame "for the joy that was set before him" (Heb. 12:2). Our earthly troubles are puny and insignificant when compared to the joys of eternal fellowship with the Father.

2. *"For a Moment"*—The second way Paul described earthly affliction was "but for a moment" (v. 17). The word *moment* means brief or for a slight period of time. Paul had developed his inward man to the place that trouble here on earth was seen as brief or for a moment. There are two reasons Paul as he did.

A. *Compared to All Other Happy Moments*—Really, now, put the pencil to your troubles! How would your afflictions stack up against the wonderful moments you've had in the Lord? I'm sure there is no comparison. We've had more revivals than funerals, haven't we? We've been in church services more often than in hospitals, haven't we? We have sung a lot more than we have cried. Thank God for all the wonderful moments in life.

B. *Compared to Eternity Ahead*—The gain will be worth the pain! The actual time of our affliction here on earth is not worthy to be compared to the infinite length of eternity shared for God's child. The woman endures the pain of childbirth realizing it is insignificant to the years of joy as the child's mother. Paul assessed his earthly troubles and concluded that their brevity could not compare to the time of eternal bliss in glory.

What about you? Do you view with grief and pessimism the aging of your physical powers? The Scriptures say that the passing of time should increase our spiritual development. Earth's trials should drive us to our knees, thrust us into God's Word, and heighten our awareness of God's Presence and fellowship.

I went to the grocery store late one night. One of my members, whom I hadn't seen for a while, was about to enter the store. I grabbed him, hugged him, and told him how much I'd missed him. He shared a sad story with me: financial difficulties, family problems, and personal failures.

"Pastor," he moaned, "I'm the union leader at my job. I give orders to rough men, and they obey me. But I cannot handle my own wife and family. Please don't waste your time on me. There is absolutely nothing that anyone can do to help me. I have given up."

This man had reached a point where his inside resources were not adequate for his outside difficulties. He was about to faint and quit in his battle against life's trials.

Life is hard and will beat down your outward self. Concentrate on the development of your inward self. Let your ways please the Lord (Prov. 16:7). "In all thy ways acknowledge him" (Prov. 3:6). "Study to show thyself approved unto God" (2 Tim. 2:15). "Let your requests be made known unto God" (Phil. 4:6). Develop your inward resources to the point where you do not faint when adversity comes. Realize that affliction is light and brief when compared to the glory ahead for us in heaven.

How is your inward self?

6

The Judgment Seat of Christ

l Corinthians 5:10

This is a generation that seemingly does not fear the judgment. Recently, in a cartoon entitled "The Far Side," the writer presented a picture of the gates of hell with a long line of people being processed before entering. The people had their suitcases as if they were checking into some resort hotel. One of Satan's servants was seated behind a desk before the gates and was putting each guest on a computer. The caption read: "Do you want inferno or noninferno? Ha! I get a kick out of saying that to people. It's all inferno, of course." Judgment and hell are not laughing matters.

The apostle Paul gave in 2 Corinthians 5:10 the doctrine concerning the "judgment seat of Christ." After sharing wonderful consolation in verses 1-9 about hope in facing death, Paul goes on to explain the next event following death, namely, the judgment. There are several judgments mentioned in the Bible, but the one before us is the "judgment seat of Christ." Other Scriptures mentioning this important event are Romans 14:10 and 1 Corinthians 3:11-15.

Many Christian are ignorant concerning the biblical doctrine of judgment. Let us observe several principles concerning the "judgment seat of Christ."

The Schedule of the Judgment Seat of Christ

A normal question concerning this great event would be: "When does the judgment seat of Christ take place?" How does the judgment seat of Christ fit in with other events of prophecy?

The judgment seat of Christ is on a schedule, God's schedule. The Bible speaks of it being a definite time—a set day. Romans 2:16 says: "In the day when God shall judge the secrets of men by Jesus Christ according to my gospel." First Corinthians 3:13 says a day is coming when every man's work shall be made manifest: "for the day shall declare it." We are speaking here of a definite time in the future.

Today we live in a time called the "Church Age" or the day of grace. This is certainly the Laodicean age as found in Revelation 3:14-22. The next great event in world history will not be the war to end all wars. As Christians, we are expecting the dramatic, sudden return of the Lord Jesus Christ, called the rapture. According to 1 Thessalonians 4:13-17 and other Scriptures, Jesus will come again, and the "dead in Christ shall rise first: then we which are alive and remain shall be caught up together with them in the clouds, to meet the Lord in the air." Jesus comes for His bride, the church, whom He purifies and rewards through the judgment seat of Christ. In the Bible, rewards are associated with the resurrection. When Jesus returns to the earth and reveals Himself to the world in Revelation 19:8, the bride is seen to have already been married and rewarded.

Therefore, the judgment seat of Christ takes place between the rapture of the church and the revelation of Christ to the earth. This purifying and rewarding of the bride will be immediately following the translation of the church out of this earth's sphere.

The Subjects of the Judgment Seat of Christ

Our text says, "We must all appear." Who is *we*?

It is clear that the judgment seat of Christ is associated only with believers. Please notice in the preceding and succeeding verses the excessive use of the words *for* and *therefore*. This entire passage is interrelated and connected. We must consider the preceding verses to determine the subjects of the judgment seat of Christ. Upon doing this, it will be clearly determined that only believers are present at this judgment.

In verse 1 the subject has an eternal home in heaven. Surely this would not refer to lost people but to saved people. In verse 2 the subject has a heavenly pull, a desire to go to heaven. Only Christians have that spiritual yearning to go to heaven!

In verse 5 the subject has received the Holy Spirit as a down payment, an "earnest" of his heavenly inheritance. Only believers possess the Holy Spirit (Rom. 8:9).

In verse 7 the subject walks by faith. We know that the lost world walks by sight. The just live and walk by faith.

In verse 8 the subjects are so submitted to God they are willing to be called to heaven if that would be best. Lost people have no desire to leave this earth! They live to increase their kingdoms here and now.

In verse 9 the subject's main ambition or desire is to be pleasing to God. Lost people do not care what God thinks. They live to please and gratify self, not God!

Thus, it should be abundantly clear that the subjects at the judgment seat of Christ are believers: the church. We must not confuse this judgment with the great white throne judgment found in Revelation 20:11-15. That judgment will be reserved exclusively for lost people, not saved people. The judgment for saved people will be the judgment seat of Christ.

The Superior at the Judgment Seat of Christ

What is the identity of the Judge presiding over this judgment? We believe the scriptural evidence sufficiently identifies our Lord Jesus as the Superior at the judgment of the believers.

Paul writes in 1 Timothy 4:1 that Jesus will judge the "quick and the dead at his appearing and his kingdom." Paul had earlier said in his famous sermon on Mars Hill that God has appointed a day in which He will judge the world in righteousness "by that man whom he hath ordained" (Acts 17:31). And then, Jesus Himself said, "The Father judgeth no man, but hath committed all judgment unto the Son" (John 5:22). It is conclusive! Jesus is the Superior.

We read today of the corruption that has infected the respected profession of judges. People are concerned about integrity and character of the ones dispensing justice in our land. When I was a boy, my parents got a divorce. I shall carry the picture of the judge who tried that case forever in my mind—the judge whittled during the trial!

We should, however, be thrilled at the identity of the Judge at the judgment seat of Christ. He is the One Who knows us. He made us. He lived on this earth Himself and was "in all points tempted like as we are" (Heb. 4:15). He is the Son of man and the "righteous judge" (2 Tim. 4:8).

Our Judge will be the One whose head and hair is white as snow and wool. His eyes are as flames of fire. His feet resemble fine brass. His voice is like the sound of many waters. Out of his mouth goes a sharp two-edged sword. This Judge's countenance is like the sun shining in its strength. These characteristics of our glorified Christ as perfect Judge are found in Revelation 1:12-16. Jesus will be the Superior.

The Summons to the Judgment Seat of Christ

Have you ever received a summons to appear in court? Our text says that "we must all appear." Attendance to the judgment seat of Christ for the believer is compulsory! I have received parking or speeding tickets and have simply sent the amount required by the ticket. This enabled me to miss the appointed court appearance. Not so with the judgment seat of Christ! There is a sense of the imperative with little word *dei*, translated "must." We *must* appear!

Also, please notice that "we must *all* appear." The attendance is universal—no exceptions! It will be "all" and yet "each." There will be a great multitude , yet no one will be lost in the crowd. We will be conscious of a multitude no one can number , yet we will be impressed by our own individuality.

In addition, examine the phrase "appear before." This implies a face-to-face meeting. It will be a personal time between us and the Judge.

Paul referred to the "judgment seat" as the *bema*. From a Roman viewpoint, the *bema* was a place where judgment was given. It was a raised place mounted by steps, a platform, a dais, a tribune. Resembling a throne, the *bema,* to the Roman was the seat of the presiding officer. From a Greek viewpoint, however, the *bema* could have referred to a nonjudicial seat of the umpire or president of the Olympic games. Here the presiding officer reviewed all the contestants and rewarded all the winners.

The apostle Paul certainly knew firsthand about the *bema*. He was brought to the *bema* at Corinth in Acts 18:12. Also the great missionary would eventually appear before Festus at the *bema* in Caesarea. He knew what it was to be summoned to the judgment seat. One day all of us Christians will answer the summons to appear before Christ at the judgment seat. "But know thou, that for all these things, God will bring thee into judgment" (Eccl. 11:9).

The Significance of the Judgment Seat of Christ

What is the purpose of the judgment seat of Christ?

Remember that we have already determined that only Christians will appear at this judgment. That tells us something very important: this judgment is not to determine whether one goes to heaven or hell. One's destiny is determined by the person at the time of departure from this earth. One must be saved and have the new nature (see vv. 5-7) before death! The judgment of heaven versus hell (one's eternal destiny) is determined by our response to the gospel here on earth. We are locked in at the time of death to our final abode by whether we are saved or lost.

The judgment seat of Christ, then, is concerned with "things done in [the] body." In other words, this judgment will be an assessment of works, not an assignment of destiny. Jesus will be dispensing rewards, not status. There are three things the judgment seat of Christ will do:

1. *Review*—Today, in the computer generation, millions of facts of information can be stored in a computer. These facts can be recalled at any time for a review—at a split second! Today we have the membership of our church on computer. I cannot tell you the times when I would spend hours searching through a Rolodex of our

church roll. Today any piece of information about any member can be instantly reviewed by use of the miraculous computer.

In addition, the technological phenomena of instant replay has revolutionized sports. The cameras roll as a game is in progress, but if needed, a scene or incident can be replayed and reviewed instantly! A fight broke out several years between the basketball teams of the Boston Celtics and the Atlanta Hawks. A player, Danny Ainge, came out of that brawl with a severely cut finger that required several stitches to close. He claimed he had been bitten by the huge Atlanta center, Tree Rollins. Rollins denied biting Danny Ainge. In the replay, however, at the bottom of the pile, the camera clearly caught Tree Rollins with Danny Ainge's finger in his mouth!

Did you know that God has all of our lives on "computer"? And He is able to instantly replay and review each life. What is God looking for as He reviews our lives? Isaiah 66:18 says that God knows our works and thoughts. Matthew 12:36 says that every idle word will be held accountable at the judgment. Romans 2:16 mentions the secrets of men. First Corinthians 4:5 announces that God will bring to light even the counsels of our hearts!

The judgment seat of Christ will, first of all, review our lives. God will look at our works, words, thoughts, secrets, and intents of our hearts. What a great God we have!

2. *Reveal*—Something wild and wonderful is happening in Florida! A man has invented a televised tombstone where a ten-minute video can be seen at the grave site simply by pushing a button on the tombstone. The inventor said he saw a grave of a man who had lived to be 107 years of age. He wondered about that man: who he was, his political affiliations, his children, and his faith. So, for

$6,000 a person can have a televised tombstone where passing people can see a video of the life of the deceased.

That brings up a question: What would you put on your life's video? Would you really tell it like it was? Would you show the good and the bad?

God's "computer" will divide one's life into good and bad. There will be a review concerning the things done in the body. Then there will also be a revelation about how the body was used. A person's real character will be revealed by the judgment seat of Christ.

The judgment will be revealing the quality of life's actions into terms called "good" and "bad." It is interesting that the word used for *bad* does not denote evil or inherent sinfulness. The word used means worthless, no account, and unable to stand the test of eternal values. It is difficult to describe the meaning of "good" because the Bible says that there is "none" who does "good, no, not one" (Rom. 3:12). The works done in this lifetime, called "good," that will stand the test of eternity may be described in this way:

A. Love—First Corinthians 13 states the importance of God's love motivating our works. Even if we give all that we have to the poor and offer ourselves as a martyr—if that were not based on God's love in our hearts, it will not stand the test of the judgment seat of Christ.

B. Faith—Hebrews 11:6 says that "without faith it is impossible to please him." Were our works based on faith? Did we walk by faith or by sight? If faith did not govern our lives, much will be lost at the judgment seat of Christ.

C. Glory—"Whatsoever ye do, do all to the glory of God" (1 Cor. 10:31). So much of what we do is for self, isn't it? Have you ever tried to look honestly at your actions to see whether God is glorified by what you do? Probably most of our "good" is by unconscious influence like the shadow ministry of Peter (Acts 5:15). Only what has been done through the Spirit and for the glory of God will stand the test at the judgment seat of Christ.

It might be helpful at this point to compare the principles studied thus far with Paul's teaching in 1 Corinthians 3:11-15. You will note there that one's lifetime works are divided into two categories: gold, silver, and precious stones or hay, wood, and stubble. In other words, our "good" works, or those who have done by love, faith, and for God's glory, are compared to precious stones. Those works of ours which have been without faith and love will be like hay, wood, and stubble. Fire is the great revealer as all the works pass through the judgment flame. Precious metals are not consumed by fire but purified. Of course, the hay, wood, and stubble are instantly consumed.

I saw Paul's description of the judgment seat of Christ vividly illustrated at a Nashville jeweler's shop. A man excitedly entered the store exclaiming that he had found a bucket of gold fillings in his grandfather's old house. The house hadn't been used in decades, and, certainly, these must be worth a fortune. The jeweler calmly said, "Well, let's give it a test to see if you've got the real thing." He reached under the counter and pulled out a little vial. He inserted an eyedropper into the vial, extracted some of the liquid, and put a drop on some shavings from the "bucket of gold." What happened next I shall never forget! There was a puff of smoke, and the gold turned green and then to ashes. "Congratulations," proclaimed the jeweler," You have a bucket full of iron filings!" I had just seen the judgment seat of Christ illustrated before my very eyes. The jeweler had used acid to reveal what sort of materials the fillings were. One day our works will be given the acid test! Only the good will remain after the judgment fire.

3. *Reward*—Not only will there be a review and revelation at the judgment seat, but there will also be a time of reward. Much is said in the Bible about the subject of rewards. Jesus told several parables illustrating the time of reward for the faithful servants. It is exciting to read: "For the Son of man shall come in the glory of his Father with his angels; and then he shall reward every man according to his works" (Matt. 16:27).

When we think of reward in this life we normally think of material rewards. Our church has a Christian school which sponsors a "No TV Week" each year. If children can go an entire week without watching television, they are rewarded with a trip to a local swimming pool on the last day of school. This is the way we envision rewards in this life.

Material goods will not be fit rewards in heaven. "The deal of the century" will not be attractive to us when we are with Jesus and our loved ones in glory! Our great joy and reward will be that we have honored and pleased Christ. Before my father-in-law passed away, we had an emotional and nostalgic family conversation. Our patriarch, Dr. Tallant, went around the family circle and praised each member for what he or she had become. Believe me, the praise and commendation were worth far more than monetary or material reward! I shall bask in the warmth of that spiritual reward until my Heavenly Father says: "Well done, thou good and faithful servant." (Matt. 25:21).

Suggestions for the Judgment Seat of Christ

We should be impressed by the solemnity of the judgment seat of Christ. "It is a fearful thing to fall into the hands of the living God" (Heb. 10:31). The judgment is no laughing or joking matter. When that time comes, every mouth will be stopped and all the world will become guilty before God (Rom. 3:19). While the judgment will be fair to all, let me remind you that "there is nothing covered, that shall not be revealed; and hid, that shall not be known" (Matt. 10:26). We should be impressed by the solemnity of the judgment seat of Christ.

How should knowing this great Bible doctrine and its certain coming affect our lives? May I suggest two scriptural applications concerning the judgment seat of Christ. Both are found near our text:

1. *We Should Want to Please God*—Verse 9 says that our desire should be to be "accepted of him." This means we want to please God by our lives or deaths. Oh, if I could live my life over again, I know I would make a better son to my parents! I remember some of the awful acts I did as a youth that broke my parents' hearts. I honestly believe that, if I could live my life over again knowing what I know now, I would not ever get a whipping! I would want to please my parents.

The judgment seat of Christ should make us want to please God. We should live clean, godly, obedient, and productive lives. We should want love to motivate all our actions. We should want to live by faith. More than anything, we would live to the glory of God. Someone has said: "Your life is God's gift to you. What you do with it is your gift to God."

2. *We Should Want to Persuade Men*—Verse 11 says, "Knowing therefore the terror of the Lord, we persuade men." A correct understanding of the judgment seat of Christ should motivate us to be fervent witnesses to the saved and lost. Knowing that our loved ones and friends will one day stand before God should compel us to be

faithful in sharing the gospel. Certainly the "love of Christ constraineth us" (v. 14), but, also, the certain judgment of God should drive us to be faithful in soul-winning. When was the last time you spoke to someone about his or her soul?

A godly Christian spoke to a young man about his soul. The conversation went something like this:

"What are you going to do when you graduate?"

"Practice law."

"Then what?"

"I hope to make a lot of money and get rich."

"Then what?"

"I hope to one day be able to retire comfortably."

"Then what?"

"I suppose I will die."

"Then what?"

His lip began to quiver, "The judgment?"

We *must* all . . . we must *all* appear . . . we must all appear before *the judgment seat of Christ. ALL.*

7
"Finish, Then, Thy New Creation"

2 Corinthians 5:17

What would you consider to be the greatest miracle of Jesus? Would it be the time He walked on the water? The raising of Lazarus from the dead? Or would it be when He fed five thousand men (not counting children and women) with a small lunch? Which wonderful miracle do you believe was Christ's most spectacular?

Many feel that the greatest miracle of our Lord was the twelve disciples. The disciples came from different walks of life: fishermen, zealots, tax collectors, and ordinary citizens. Yet, these "dirty dozen" were transformed into dynamic disciples of Christ. Jesus literally poured Himself into them over a space of three years. These disciples took His words, learned from His example, and caught Christ's vision to give the gospel to the world. Truly, the twelve disciples can only be explained as new creatures in Christ.

The seventeenth verse of 2 Corinthians 5 literally explodes off the Bible page: "Therefore if any man be in Christ, he is a new creature: old things are passed away; behold, all things are become new." Only Christianity could make such a marvelous claim: "a new creature." Only through Jesus Christ can a person receive a new start in life. God's Word promises that we can become "new creature[s].

Before listing several ways in which a child of God becomes new, notice several key words of Paul in verse 17. The phrase "in Christ" is one of Paul's favorite phrases. Found 160 times in the apostle's writings, "in Christ" describes one's union with Christ. One's relationship and security in Christ are portrayed by Paul when he used this phrase. It is interesting that our word *archaic* comes from the word Paul used for "old." The meaning of "new" gives us the picture of freshness and total change. The tense of the verb in verse 17 implies that one remains new.

We are promised to be "new" when we are in Christ. Let us examine some of the new positions and possessions given to the child of God:

A New Nature

The most obvious change in us upon receiving Christ as Savior is that we have a new nature. The words *new creation* speak of this new nature.

Most vividly the Scriptures speak of our *lives* before Christ: "conversation in times past in the lusts of our flesh, fulfilling the desires of the flesh and of the mind; and were by nature the children of wrath" (Eph. 2:3). We were controlled by Satan (Eph. 2:2). All of us were declared "dead in trespasses and sins" before finding Christ (Eph. 2:1). But the power of the gospel "quickens" us- ,makes us alive! God is not just our Creator, but now becomes our Heavenly Father (Rom. 8:15). It is by our new spiritual nature that we cry "Abba, Father" (Rom. 8:15).

Through our new nature, we have changed families. Before Christ we were in the family of Adam. "As in Adam all die" (1 Cor. 15:22). By the new birth (John 3:3), we have been placed in the family of Christ: "even so in

Christ shall all be made alive" (1 Cor. 15:22). We now possess the nature of Christ, "partakers of the divine nature" (2 Pet. 1:4).

Have you ever seen an orange tree planted from an orange seed? No, you have not! The miracle of the orange tree doesn't work that way. I was raised in central Florida and worked as a laborer in the orange groves most of my youth. The productive orange tree began as a lemon or sour orange seedling. At a certain age, this seedling is "budded" as life from a productive orange is engrafted into its bark. This new life literally transforms the sour orange or lemon into a fresh fruit tree full of the promise of sweetness. Without the new nature, the seedling would develop as a sour orange producing undesirable fruit.

In like manner, when we become "in Christ," we receive a new nature enabling us to produce fruit acceptable to God. Without our new natures, our lives cannot please God or be a blessing to humankind. Thank God for our new nature!

A New Name

How thrilled I was to give my name to my wife when we married! I know that it must please God to give us a new name when we become new creatures in Christ. Notice some of these names:

*We are now called "Christians" (Acts 11:26). Probably this was a term of derision at its inception. Today it may have become a generic term because everyone has a different idea of the term "Christian." It literally means, "little Christ." We should be proud that when people see us they think of Christ. Every believer today has "Christian" as his or her official last name: Billie Friel Christian.

*We are also called the children of God (John 1:12).

When we receive Christ, we are given the power or right to become God's children. God is now our Heavenly Father, and we are His children.

*A third prominent name given to the new creature in Christ is that of saint (1 Cor. 1:2). This name does not imply that our lives have attained such greatness in Christ that we are immortalized as legends. The root word for saint involves holiness. Because God is holy, and we now have His nature in us, we are classified as holy or "saints."

Many of God's children received new Christian names. Simon was elevated to Peter. Saul became Paul. The apostles saw the spiritual gift of exhortation in Joses and named him Barnabas (Acts 4:36). May we wear proudly the new names of Christian, child of God, and saint.

A New Nemesis

It is amazing how ignorant we were to Satan's activity in our lives before responding to the gospel! Satan was there all the time blinding us, but we did not apprehend his presence. No, not until we were quickened in the Spirit did we become aware of a nemesis to our life in Christ.

Paul has presented a most vivid treatise on the doctrine of Satan in Second Corinthians. He called him the "god of this world" in 4:4. Satan was called a beguiler in 11:3. Then he was labeled an "angel of light" in 11:14. The apostle knew what would happen to the person who became a "new creature" in Christ. He would become aware of a deadly enemy whose nature is that of a murderer, liar, thief, and accuser of the brethren.

Wonder why we are not sensitive to Satan's operations when we are outside of Christ? Once there was a godly sharecropper whose boss was a skeptical unbeliever.

These two would have deep discussions about the Christian faith. Once they were considering the existence of Satan while the boss hunted ducks. The old farmhand could not convince his owner about Satan's presence. Suddenly, a group of ducks flew overhead. The boss fired several times and wounded one of the ducks.

"Quick! Go get that one before he gets away!" hollered the boss.

The Christian hand returned with a grin on his face. "You're not worried about those ducks that are dead, are you? That's the way it is with old Satan and people. He don't bother those who are dead. But, once you become alive in the Lord, then you feel the devil fighting against you!"

In like manner, the "new creature" in Christ becomes aware of a new nemesis. He or she is sensitive to the presence of Satan.

A New Nucleus

A nucleus is defined as a central part around which other parts are grouped. Further, it means a center of development or growth.

What a superb definition of the church! The church becomes for the new Christian a central part around which we group, grow, and develop. The church is not a club or fraternal order after the worldly fashion. We, who have been saved, can testify to the natural rallying we do to our spiritual family. It has been so since the foundation of the church:

* "The multitude of them that believed were of one heart and of one soul: neither said any of them that ought of the things which he possessed was his own; but they had all things common" (Acts 4:32).

* "All that believed were together, and had all things common" (Acts 2:44).

The new nucleus of a Christian is beautifully illustrated by the early church. Acts 2:46-47 says the believers continued with one accord in the Temple. The new nucleus broke bread from house to house and ate with gladness and singleness of heart. These were people mainly from the Jewish religion who had found a new nucleus in Christ.

Do you remember the tabernacle? Whether on the move or at rest, the tabernacle was always at the center of the Israelite camp. God so ordained that each tribe would have its set place around the tabernacle, whether on the march or at rest. The tabernacle was always at the center of the camp. All paths led to the house of God.

For the "new creature" in Christ, the church becomes the center of his or her life, doesn't it? One's spiritual nucleus becomes closer than actual blood kin in many cases. Happy is the family whose lives group, grow, and develop around their spiritual nucleus, the Church.

A young lady in our church was having problems. Soon she committed herself into an institution specializing in addiction rehabilitation. We could not visit her for the first ten days while she became acclimated to the program. I shall never forget going to the institution to see her. My wife and I were thrilled to see that she had gained weight, taken on a rosy complexion once again, and was genuinely happy. Throughout our conversation, this beautiful young mother repeated these phrases to us: "My pills were my gods . . . I have to change my playgrounds and my playmates."

How similar this experience applies to the child of God! Each of us can attest to the inward desire upon being saved to change our playground and playmates. We have the nature of God in us and this compels us to seek a new nucleus, the church.

A New Nutrition

The new creatures in Christ soon make a remarkable discovery! They crave a new nutrition. The new nature demands new food and sustenance. There are two verses of Scripture that describe this new nutrition:

* "It is written, Man shall not live by bread alone, but by every word that proceedeth out of the mouth of God" (Matt. 4:4).

* "As newborn babes, desire the sincere milk of the word, that ye may grow thereby" (1 Pet. 2:2).

The Word of God becomes absolutely indispensable to the newborn child of God. A new nature has been implanted, and it must be nourished. Only the Word of God can give vital strength and nourishment to our new nature. There is something about us now that food can't feed, money can't buy, sex can't satisfy, and clothes can't clothe. It is the very nature of God in us.

How often we have witnessed the spiritual growth of new converts. If involved in a regular Bible study immediately following conversion, the new convert takes to the "pablum" of God's Word like a little baby to baby food! It is thrilling to hear young Christians testify as to the works and Words of God in them. His hunger for the Word of God is like tearing a page from the Book of Acts! When we examine the early church we find the process the same: "received his word . . . baptized . . . continued steadfastly in the apostles' doctrine" (Acts 2:41-42). After salvation comes nutrition.

Just like physical babies, our natures begin with the "milk of the word" (1 Pet. 2:2). We must learn the basics of the Bible: how to pray, to confess, to study, to worship, and apply the Word to beginning areas of our lives. Our goal is to graduate to "strong meat" in the Word of God (Heb. 5:12-14). As we mature and develop in the Word, we have our "senses exercised to discern both good and evil" (Heb. 5:14).

If I had to ask you one question to determine your spiritual IQ, it would not be concerning your prayer life, church attendance, or visitation participation. It would be: "How much time do you spend in the study of God's Word?" Without our spiritual nutrition, we become emaciated spiritually. Without the nutrition from God's Word, we become spiritual anemics. Are you taking your spiritual nutrition?

A New Necessity

Another discovery is made by the new creatures in Christ: they finds a new desire for Christian duty and service. In our text, Paul says that the new creature in Christ is given the "ministry of reconciliation" (v. 18). To the child of God is committed the "word of reconciliation" (v. 19). Because we have become reconciled to God, we have the necessity to help others find peace with God. It is my personal opinion that the children of God will actually have to force themselves *not* to speak freely about their newfound life in Christ. The new creatures will almost have to backslide if they keep quiet about their ministry of reconciliation! What I am emphasizing is: the new life in Christ brings about the new necessity to share the gospel with others.

Remember King David's autobiographical fifty-first Psalm? David had sinned against God, Uriah, and Bathsheba. More than anything he desired a clean heart and a right spirit (v. 10). How he wanted to be close to God again

(v. 11). He knew that he was missing the joy of his salvation (v. 12). When all of these spiritual elements were back in David's life, what would happen? "Then will I teach transgressors thy ways; and sinners shall be converted unto thee" (v. 13). When we are right with God, we have a new necessity!

Different motives stir this new necessity. Second Corinthians 5:11 states that we persuade people because of the terror of the Lord. The love of Christ constrains us as found in verse 14. Both of these motives will affect you at different times to share Christ. One thing is sure, however, and that is: we are our brother's keeper!

A couple was staying in a large downtown hotel during a business convention. One night the wife decided to go down to lobby and observe the people of the city. Soon she came back to the room and was noticeably disturbed. She told her husband: "I just had the most shocking experience. A man came up to me in the lobby and asked if I were saved." Her husband replied, "I hope you told him that you were a member of the church, didn't you? that you taught a Sunday School class for many years? that you sang each Sunday in the choir?" The woman said, "He didn't ask me that. He asked me if I were saved." Her husband again defended her by stating, "I guess you told him it was none of his business, didn't you?"

To this the spiritually awakened wife said: "If you had seen the look on his face and heard the tone of his voice, you would have known it was his business!" We have the Word and the ministry of reconciliation. This is a new necessity in our lives: to tell others about Jesus.

What about you? Are you a new creature in Christ Jesus? If so, then you will have a new nature, a new name, a new nemesis, a new nucleus, a new nutrition, and a new necessity. Life for you is truly new.

8
A Model Stewardship Church

2 Corinthians 8

Since I am a pastor, guess which programs of the church concern me the most. Outreach and stewardship. I am always concerned about our witnessing and giving. I do not know of a pastor who feels satisfied with his programs of outreach and stewardship! We can always be more and do more for our precious Lord, can't we?

The stewardship program at the church of Corinth had the apostle Paul concerned, too. Under the inspiration of the Holy Spirit, Paul wrote the classic Bible passage on Christian stewardship as found in 2 Corinthians 8 and 9. Chapter 8 deals with church stewardship, and chapter 9 describes personal stewardship. These two chapters give us a complete summary of motives and methods concerning God's program of stewardship. If today's churches and Christians were familiar with these principles, there would be no burdens upon the pastors concerning stewardship! The treasuries would overflow.

A great need existed in the mother Church at Jerusalem. Several reasons, particular to Jerusalem, created this need. For one thing, the Jerusalem area was not blessed agriculturally as other areas in Israel. We note, also, that there was not a great material wealth potential in Jerusalem—mainly small businesses. The main reason for the need, however, came from the fact that Jerusalem

was a "pilgrim" city. Many visitors came to this sacred
city. These visitors would come in contact with the gospel,
find Christ as Savior, and then want to remain with their
new friends and family in the faith. This put a tremen-
dous financial burden upon the already strained Jerusalem church. There was a need in Jerusalem.

Paul felt a keen call to meet the need in the Jerusalem
church. He was a Jew and loved his fellow Jews. His
Christian compassion and sympathy was stirred to help.
The Jerusalem church was the "mother" church of the
gospel; therefore, the Gentile churches were grateful
debtors and should want to meet the need. But Paul saw
another reason to lead an effort by the Gentile churches
in helping Jerusalem: this project would reduce the natural suspicion of Jewish Christians for the Gentile believers. A love gift would demonstrate Christian love and
sympathy. So, Paul began to organize an effort to raise a
great offering to minister to the needs of the Jerusalem
church.

Nothing inspires a great endeavor like a good example.
In chapters 8 and 9, the apostle holds up the giving record
of the Macedonian churches to the Corinthian church.
Acts 16 and 17 contain the record of the apostle's ministry to Philippi, Berea, and Thessalonica. Truly, these
were outstanding churches, and Paul used their records
of faithfulness to inspire the Corinthian church.

Let us think about "The Measure of a Church's Giving"
as based on Paul's words in 2 Corinthians 8:

A Church's Ability

In motivating the Corinthian church, Paul first spoke
about the ability of the Macedonian churches. He used
the word *power* in verse 3. This word could be translated
"ability." "For to their power, I bear record " (v. 3). The

apostle knew firsthand the giving potential of the Macedonian churches. Paul knew the area, the people, and the true potential giving power of the churches. We can only give from what God puts into our hands. We are not expected to give what we do not have! Paul said that he could bear record of the giving ability of the churches of Macedonia, and it was not much!

This leads to an interesting question: What are the abilities or potential power of your church? What is your church capable of doing? It can be an humbling experience to take an X-ray of your church and compare its potential power with its actual performance. Let me share some indicators of a church's ability:

Attendance - In my denomination, the attendance formula is about 50 percent of the Sunday School enrollment. In other words, a church with a Sunday School enrollment of 500 would probably be averaging 220-250 in Bible Study attendance. Usually we are told that if our attendance is more than 50 percent of our enrollment, then our enrollment is too low. Has your class begun new units in the past few years? The most expensive item in our budget is empty pews—our attendance is an indicator of the church's ability.

Baptisms - Divide the number of your church's membership by the total number of baptisms. That number tells you how many members it took to win and baptize a convert. There have been times when that ratio in our state conventions was 40 to 1! Think of it! It takes forty (or more) people to baptize one convert. How we need more members trained in soul-winning and involved in outreach!

Music - I heard our minister of music say that his choir should be 10 percent of the congregation in worship. In other words, if there were three hundred in your worship attendance, your choir should have about thirty in it. Obviously there are many members who should be using their musical talents for the Lord. If I were not a pastor, I would love to sing in the choir.

Soul-Winners - I heard a noted speaker say once that there was not a church in the country that had 5 percent of its members as soul-winners. "Surely that is not true," I thought. But when I began to consider the implications at my own church, I knew he was correct. A church with a membership of five hundred would have twenty-five soul-winners—that is a good number for any church. What about your witnessing ability?

Giving - We tried something recently at our church to determine our stewardship potential. First, we contacted the Chamber of Commerce and received the actual median family income for our immediate area (a five square mile area). We took a tenth of that figure (a "legal tithe") and multiplied the answer by the number of families in our church. The answer could be interpreted as the giving potential of our people. Do you know—our present budget is only about two thirds of that figure! What is the giving ability of your church?

Once a country rooster went to the big city to visit his cousin. While there his relative took him to visit the zoo. Many of the animals impressed him, especially the ostrich. When the rooster returned to his farm, he lined up his hens and showed them an ostrich egg. He made an impassioned speech in which he said, "Ladies, I'm not trying to embarrass you or make you feel guilty. I just want you to see what other hens are doing in other places!" Paul is saying: "Dear Corinthian church, I just want you to know what God is doing with other churches." He knew the ability of the Macedonian churches.

A Church's Affliction

There was another key to the giving of the Macedonian churches that made them all the more remarkable. Paul stated that they had been enduring affliction and poverty. Notice verse 2: "great trial of affliction" and "deep poverty." These churches were not in the Bible Belt, and they were not on the most desirable church list for graduating seminary students!

The area of Macedonia had endured its share of trouble. Several civil wars had ravaged the areas which comprised these church fields. Also, when you read Acts 16 and 17, Philippians 1:29, and 1 Thessalonians 2:3-18, you note that there was a persecution of the believers. When persecution occurs, there will be the damaging of property and plundering of possessions. There had been difficult days for the Macedonian churches.

Civil wars and persecution had combined to make what little the Macedonian churches owned become pitifully small. "Poverty" presents a picture of a beggar with nothing and no hope to get anything. Paul was saying, "I know this area. I know their giving potential. What they had originally possessed was drastically reduced by civil war and persecution."

I think of some churches in South Louisiana and along the Texas coast line. Practically each year hurricanes bring fear and possible devastation to these churches. Yet, they remain true to God and the gospel in spite of being wrecked and ransacked often by great storms coming each year off the ocean. The ability of the Macedonian churches was influenced by a devastating affliction that had caused deep poverty.

A Church's Abundance

Pastors encounter all the feeble excuses concerning people's inability to give—if they live long enough! A man went next door to borrow an ax from his neighbor. His neighbor said, "I'm sorry. You can't borrow my ax because I'm having potatoes for supper." The shocked man exclaimed, "What does that have to do with me borrowing your ax?" To which the neighbor replied, "Nothing. I just don't want to loan my ax, and one excuse is as good as another!"

If any area had an "excuse" not to give; it would have been these Macedonian churches. But notice verse 2: their affliction produced joy, and their poverty resulted in liberality! Despite civil war and persecution, the Macedonians gave a magnificent offering to aid the famine victims in Jerusalem. Joy overflowed their affliction, and generosity came from their poverty.

It is not always the most wealthy who are the most generous. Often those with the least to give are the most ready to share. Several reasons make the poor people extremely usable by God:

* Poverty makes us humble—God gives grace to the humble: James 4:6; Luke 14:11.

* Poverty makes us totally dependent on God as our Source: Zechariah 4:6.

* Poverty makes us live simple and satisfied lives: 1 Timothy 6:6-8.

Studies and Internal Revenue Service reports show that the higher the income, the lower the commitment to giving. I have been audited several times by the IRS concerning my gift to the church. Although it always is a frightening experience, I was honored that I could represent my love for my Lord before the government. I have often entertained the thought that if every Christian were not audited sometime by the IRS for reported giving, then, he or she must not be an "hilarious" giver! (2 Cor. 9:7). Certainly the Macedonian Christians would have been prime suspects for a government audit. Their giving abounded in spite of great affliction and deep poverty.

A Church's Accomplishment

Paul applied the modern saying, "Put your money where your mouth is," to the Corinthian church. He had spoken to them over a year ago concerning the collection for the Jerusalem saints (1 Cor. 16:1-2). It was now time to finish what had been started (v. 6).

The apostle came down hard on the Corinthians' lack of accomplishment. He reminded them of their leadership role among the churches—see verse 7. They abounded in everything—this included faith, wonderful preachers, great teaching, zeal and enthusiasm, and devotion. Paul said: "See that ye abound in this grace also" (v. 7). He was exhorting them concerning their giving.

Paul said the accomplishment of this project would "prove the sincerity of your love" (v. 8). The Corinthian church had been more forward in words than in deeds. No words were minced: "Now therefore perform the doing of it" (v. 11). Strong words from the apostle!

Could it be that we pastors have not spiritually exhorted our people in the area of stewardship? My heart was convicted as I noted that, in this classic passage on Christian stewardship, the word *money* was never mentioned! Paul used the terms "grace" (v. 1), "liberality" (v. 2), "fellowship of the ministering" (v. 4), "supply" (v. 14), "proof of your love" (v. 24), "bountifulness" (9:11), "service" (9:12), and "liberal distribution" (9:13). How many of us pastors could preach a strong message on stewardship and never mention the word *money?*

Paul was very straightforward in his appeal. He literally said, "You know the need. You know what you ought to do. Now, do it!" Could it be that our churches need to hear an authoritative message from the pastors in the area of stewardship? I have people in my church who feel that I do not take a strong enough stand in the area of giving. One man has said, "You know who will squirm when you preach honestly and hard on money—the thieves! Go on, and do it! Those of us who love the Lord and the church, why, it doesn't bother us a bit!" Paul emphasized the need for accomplishment to the Corinthians: see verses 6, 7, 8, 10, 11, and 24.

Many people have good intentions, but these don't help the cause of Christ. Each good feeling must be put into a fine action. It is said that Mark Twain was once visiting in Africa and happened upon a Christian service in progress. Twain sat down on the back row and proceeded to listen to a most eloquent sermon by a young missionary. The famous American was impressed. *When the offering comes,*" he thought, *I'll give $100.*" The preacher emphasized his point again, prompting Twain to reason: *Well, maybe just $50.* The service continued with the heat and smells having their effects on Twain. *He's down to $10.* To make a long story short, Twain later related that the service lasted so long he stole a quarter from the offering plate!

Many of our people have a good impulse to give and then do not follow through on it. Paul would say, "Now therefore perform the doing of it" (v. 11). The apostle John would add: "My little children, let us not love in word, neither in tongue; but in deed and in truth" (1 John 3:18).

A Church's Availability

What was the secret of the Macedonian church's stewardship? How were they enabled to give a magnificent gift to meet the Jerusalem crisis in spite of great affliction and deep poverty? In our Convention today, we are thrilled to hear about great offerings for building programs. How do these happen? Is there a secret in producing dynamic givers?

There are two points that Paul made concerning a church's availability:

1. *Priority* - The bottom line of the Macedonian secret lies in the fact that they "first gave their own selves to the Lord" (v. 5). The person came before the pocketbook! When our bodies become a "living sacrifice," then God will receive our "reasonable service" (Rom. 12:1).

We have a man in our church who lived a rough, tough life. He had no use for God as he majored on eastern religions and karate. I visited him on several occasions and was kindly ushered out of the house. But God convicted him through his little boy, and soon salvation came to the entire family. One day this man called me. "Preacher, tell me about this tithing stuff. I'm ready!" I explained to him what the Old and New Testaments said about tithing. "All right," he proclaimed, "I'll start Sunday." I thought of all the times of visitation to this man's home. If I had ever mentioned giving during that time, he would have probably aimed a karate kick at my head! But, now, he has given himself to the Lord. After we give ourselves to the Master, it becomes a natural thing to share what we realize He has given to us.

2. *Willingness* - The Macedonians exemplify the epitome of Christian commitment. We should not have to beg God's children to give! Paul was ready to exempt the

churches of Macedonia from the offering for the Jerusalem saints. No sir! These churches would not hear of that!
These model believers were in such a spiritual state that
they were "Praying us with much entreaty that we would
receive the gift" (v. 4). They did not want to miss the opportunity to be a part of this great Christian venture!

Can you imagine a pastor being begged to take up an
offering? Will we ever see the time like it was in Moses'
day? The people responded so magnanimously in bringing gifts for the construction of the tabernacle that the
Scripture says: "So the people were restrained from
bringing. For the stuff they had was sufficient for all the
work to make it, and too much" (Ex. 36:6-7). Oh, I hope I
live to make the announcement to my people: "Please,
please. No more giving is necessary. We have too much in
our treasury." When our people first give themselves to
the Lord, then they will be hilariously willing to give.

A church had a great day planned to raise money for
the building program. During the service the people were
to march to the front and deposit their gift. The pastor
stopped a stooped elderly lady whom he knew was on social security. "Oh, Aunt Bertie, you don't need to give."
"But I want to give," replied the dear saint. The pastor
persisted, "I know how your funds are limited. You don't
have to give." To this the little lady hissed to her pastor,
"I must give!"

The churches of Macedonia had a "willing mind" (v.
12). I can hear them hiss to the apostle Paul: "We must
give!" They did give, and we, along with the Jerusalem
saints, are blessed because they did.

Check your church's ability to give. Realize how God
can use the members for abundance in spite of affliction
and poverty. Our churches can accomplish wonderful
ministries if they are available and willing.

9
Spiritual Warfare

2 Corinthians 10:1-6

A famous Hollywood comedian is known for the classic line: "I don't get no respect." His monologue will be punctuated again and again with this comment. For example, the comedian once said he had so much acne and pimples as a youth that a blind man tried to read his face! Whether it is his wife, children, friends, or boss—the comment is always the same: "I don't get no respect!"

The apostle Paul seemingly never received any respect from the Corinthian church, even though Paul founded the church. Divisions rocked the church. Leaders questioned Paul's authority again and again. In verse 1 we note that they accused his personal presence as "base" or "lowly." No doubt the physical presence of Paul was not impressive. His manner of leadership was labeled by the Corinthian church as almost cowardly. Some confused meekness with weakness and implied that the only time Paul showed firm leadership was when he wrote to them. Paul could have used the comedian's line: "I don't get no respect!"

There was coming a time, however, when Paul would face the leaders of this conflict. He would rather use the meekness and gentleness of Christ in dealing with them.

If that were not possible, then Paul would exercise bold-ness and would decisively challenge them. Paul herewith sent them his challenge in advance.

Paul then gave a true explanation concerning the na-ture of church conflict. He had seen it as spiritual war-fare. It is as if we are given a spiritual X-ray of the church and are shown the way God views the conflict surround-ing the gospel.

The apostle knew the Roman army well, and once again he effectively used the military metaphor. Picture, if you will, the Roman army defeating nation after nation and then incorporating them into the empire. Imagine what it meant to conquer a nation and then make them "Roman." We remember that the city of Philippi was like a little Rome: the citizens lived under Roman laws and were taught to think as Romans. Conquest according to Roman standards was not only to assault and defeat the strongholds of resistance. It also involved bringing into captivity each member of the defeated nation and totally absorbing them into the Roman Empire.

Paul's knowledge of the methods of the Roman con-quest will now be vividly portrayed as he discusses spiri-tual warfare.

Life as a Warfare

In many ways most Christians of today are anemic when compared to the biblical standard of Christianity. The attributes of boldness, generosity, and sacrifice seem foreign to the life-style of today's believer. Nowhere more than in the area of spiritual warfare do we see the diver-gence from biblical Christianity. The average church member of today is ignorant about the doctrine of spiritual warfare. Today's professor of Christ thinks the Christian life centers around the playground, not a battleground! This view would be foreign to the theology of the apostle Paul. He called the believers "soldier[s]" and exhorted them to endure hardness (2 Tim. 2:3) Looking back over his ministry, Paul concluded that he had "fought a good fight" (2 Tim. 4:7). Let us underscore the fact that the gospel life is not a playground but a battleground!

In 2 Corinthians 10:4, Paul referred to "our warfare." The word for warfare is *strategia*. This Greek word is found only here and in 1 Corinthians 9:7 and 1 Timothy 1:18, where Timothy is urged to "war a good warfare." *Strategia* does not refer merely to a skirmish or short tiff but to a campaign. Paul saw the entire sphere of spiritual warfare and called it a campaign. It is literally a lifelong battle.

There is a massive, full-scale campaign being waged over human souls:

* Satan is the commander-in-chief of an army opposing God and His people.

* Satan has a powerful army composed of super beings called demons. These demons participated with Satan in a revolt in heaven. They were cast out of heaven with their master, Satan (Rev. 12:7-9). Today these demons carry out the wishes of Satan.

* Satan has devices or schemes to overthrow the kingdom of God (2 Cor. 2:11).

* Satan has fiery darts which he hurls at each Christian (see Eph. 6:16). This ruler of evil knows our weaknesses, our Achilles's heels. He is able to hit us at the right time with a temptation calculated to make us choose disobedience instead of obedience.

* Since the Fall (Gen. 3), each person who has lived

must be "won" to faith in Jesus Christ (Prov. 11:30). Satan has ruled every soul, and he has had to be attacked and made to relinquish his hold.

* Satan is after every Christian, every Christian home, every Christian church, and every Christian denomination. There is a spiritual warfare going on in the world! This is not a physical warfare but a spiritual warfare. Notice Paul's emphasis on "imaginations," "high thing," and "thought" in 2 Corinthians 10:5. Verse 3 says: "For though we walk in the flesh, we do not war after the flesh." Paul would impress upon us, first of all, that the Christian life is a spiritual warfare.

Strongholds to Capture

The spiritual warfare involves capturing strongholds. The word "strongholds" in the New Testament is found only here in 2 Corinthians 10:4. It refers to a formidable fortification. The closest equivalent to it in modern times might be the "pillbox" of World War II. The enemy would have a fortification located on a strategically elevated spot where such a position could control an entire area. That fortification would have to be stormed, sometimes at dreadful cost, for our troops to forge ahead. The concept of "stronghold" or fortification may be difficult for our modern-day minds to grasp. We're probably as ignorant as the fellow entering the army. The old boy simply could not understand the military terminology. Once he was publicly asked to define a "fortification." The boy scratched his head and replied, "Well, Sarge, I guess a fortification would be two twentifications!"

The Roman army liked to operate from the high ground, if possible. The stronghold could have been a tower or a huge pile of earth or brush from which a strong defense was made. One of the most formidable strongholds you might remember is Masada by the Dead Sea. If the enemy ever made it to the top of Masada, there was little chance to defeat him. You may also remember the tragic story of the Jewish settlement which decided to perish there.

Paul applied the theme of spiritual warfare to the vivid military concepts. He said in verse 5 that there are spiritual strongholds which exalt themselves against the knowledge of God. These are spiritual strongholds which must be pulled "down." The words "*pulling down*" and "*casting down*" in verses 4 and 5 are action words and are described in other passages. In Luke 12:18 the rich fool said he had so much that he was going to "pull down" his present barns and build greater ones. We see that the words would mean to dismantle, destroy, or pull down. These spiritual strongholds must be destroyed or dismantled before one can have a victorious Christian life.

Let me name some spiritual strongholds of today:

* Reasonings that are opposed to God's truth—the word *imaginations* could be translated "reasonings."

* Intellectualism—Here Paul refers to high-minded attitudes by people who think they know more than they really do.

* Worldliness and Materialism—This is the mistaken idea that wealth can buy anything and take one anywhere. People are so in love with this world that they do not realize preparation must be made for eternity.

* Cults—Consider groups of false worshippers where the basic tenets of the gospel of Jesus Christ (1 Cor. 15:3-4) are not believed and followed. Usually such strongholds do not teach a personal experience with Christ for salvation or that the Bible is the Word of God.

* Occult strongholds exist as people worship Satan and enter the bondage of demonic habits.

* Strongholds of selfishness and pride are in every heart as resistance toward Christ. Remember the rich man's vocabulary: "I," "my fruits," "my barns," and "my goods" (Luke 12:17-18).

Whatever opposes itself against the knowledge of Christ can be considered a stronghold. These strongholds must be pulled down if we are to live a victorious Christian life.

The next logical question would be: "How are these strongholds pulled down?"

Weapons of Our Warfare

To fight a war, one must have weapons.

Notice in verse 3 that we do not "war after the flesh." Also, in verse 4 we recognize that the weapons of our warfare are not "carnal." Carnal means of the flesh or physical.

Paul's adversaries in the church at Corinth used fleshly or carnal weapons. There were personality contests: camps favoring Paul, some for Peter, and others for Apollos. Human abilities, rather than spiritual gifts, were being emphasized. Scheming had taken the place of prayer. People were being manipulated. Satan also effectively used slander and gossip as two weapons to create perpetual conflict in the church.

The battle for human souls, however, goes deeper than that! We cannot fight spiritual battles with carnal weapons. We cannot use human weapons to defeat demonic forces.

How weapons have changed throughout the history of humanity! We remember the clubs of the cave dwellers. Swords and knives made it easier to kill people. Then bows, arrows, and spears enabled people to kill from a distance. Ball-and-powder muskets changed the art of warfare! Modern-day rifles and artillery were invented, and people could be killed by the enemy thousands of feet from the scene. Now we are confronted by nuclear devices that boggle the mind. How will weaponry continue to change? Light rays and laser weapons? Only time will prevent weapons from reaching shocking sophistication.

Can you imagine the caveman with his club trying to wage war against the rocketry of today? It would be no contest! In like manner, we will fail if we use fleshly weapons against demonic powers.

The strongholds must be assaulted and captured by weapons that are "mighty through God" (v. 4). The word "mighty" is *dunata* and refers to a force powerful enough to capture these spiritual strongholds. These weapons are spiritually equipped for the purpose of waging a successful warfare against demonic beings from the underworld.

We can praise God that the gospel is the "power of God unto salvation" (Rom. 1:16). Every excuse and reasoning against the gospel will eventually be cast down!

It has been noted that our weapons are not fleshly but spiritual and mighty through God. What are some of these spiritual weapons God uses to assault and capture the strongholds of the enemy?

1. *The Preaching of the Cross*—We know the "preaching of the cross is to them that perish foolishness; but unto us which are saved it is the power of God" (1 Cor. 1.18). The story of Jesus—coming to earth, born of a virgin, living a sinless life, dying for the sins of the world, being buried, miraculously raised from the dead, and ascending to heaven—is not a fantasy! The gospel story is a fantastic fact which God blesses when proclaimed clearly and in the power of the Holy Spirit.

A young couple visited our church who had been addicted to alcohol and drugs. They had been faithfully attending a rehabilitation center where human methods were used to contain the demonic habits of addictive substances. Two men from our church visited this precious couple, and, in the course of their visit, mentioned the name of Jesus several times. The young couple had never heard how to reach God through Jesus. They had believed in as much of the "higher power" as they knew, but they did not have true peace and relief. It was not until they called upon the name of Jesus (Jas. 2:19; Rom. 10:13) that a Power greater than drugs came into their lives. The gospel is a fantastic spiritual weapon!

2. *The Word of God*—The Word of God is the "sword of the Spirit" (Eph. 6:17). The Word is "quick, and powerful" (Heb. 4:12). Jesus said that His words were "spirit" and "life" (John 6:63). Let us memorize the Scriptures faithfully because God will use them through us to pull down strongholds.

A brilliant infidel went to hear a famous evangelist with the express purpose of criticizing his speech. The evangelist had not graduated from high school and was known for grammatical errors in his delivery. However, the evangelist had memorized hundreds of Scriptures (which are grammatically correct!), and that night he quoted many of them. The infidel was wonderfully converted and confessed later that the evangelist touched him by hiding behind the Scriptures! God's Word is a great weapon.

3. *Prayer*—Our prayers reach God, and God changes people. Prayer was used by God to open prison doors for Peter (Acts 12:5). It was at a prayer meeting that Lydia's heart was opened (Acts 16:13-15). We can all testify that "effectual fervent prayer" avails much (Jas. 5:16).

When I was saved, a small group of ladies were praying for me each night of the revival. God, through those prayers, made a "good boy" realize he was a sinner. When the people of God begin to travail in prayer, children are born. (Isa. 66:8).

4. *Love*—What a mysteriously powerful weapon love is! There have been rough, tough men who have been won to salvation because someone loved them to Jesus. Certainly the love Stephen demonstrated toward his enemies made an impression of the heart of young Saul (Acts 7:58-60). "Charity never faileth" (1 Cor. 13:8). Keep loving that person! You may be tempted to give up, but, remember, love "beareth all things, believeth all things, hopeth all things, endureth all things" (1 Cor. 13:7).

A big strong man once gave a testimony concerning his salvation. He said that what broke him was the love the men of our church showed for him. Listen! You may not have all the answers, but you can love a person! And love "shall cover the multitude of sins" (1 Pet. 4:8). Love is a great spiritual weapon.

5. *Submission*—How the world misunderstands the biblical doctrine of submission. Submission does not mean one becomes a punching bag or doormat. It means to voluntarily rank oneself under the authority of another. The wife of an unbelieving husband is urged to be submissive, and God will use this to win her husband! (1 Pet. 3:1).

We have a man in our church who was so hard to reach for Jesus. He testified that the turning point came when his wife was saved. She became so loving and so submissive he could not resist finding her God! Some women are more intelligent than their husbands and have more appealing personalities, but when wives voluntarily submit to their husbands, as unto the Lord, salvation often comes to their mates (Eph. 5:22).

These are five spiritual weapons that are "mighty through God to the pulling down of strongholds" (2 Cor. 10:4).

The Objective of Our Warfare

Physical warfare is cruel, brutal, and devastating. The Roman army, which Paul used as an example, left no resistance. Captives were either executed or made thoroughly Roman.

Let us retrace the military metaphor Paul has been using. The Roman army was on the march. Blocking the path of the army was an enemy stronghold or fortification. Special weapons and fighting instruments were brought to deal specifically with that stronghold. Soon these specially equipped weapons (battering rams, catapults, etc.) had weakened the stronghold sufficiently to allow the attacking soldiers to pull it down. The enemy soldiers were taken captive and either executed or Romanized, so they were never again a threat to the Roman Empire.

In examining the day-to-day life of the believer, Paul stresses that we are engaged in spiritual warfare. As we attempt to march victoriously with the gospel, we will encounter strongholds of resistance which are energized by Satan himself. We cannot use physical weapons to fight superior spiritual foes. Our weapons must be spiritual and mighty through God to the pulling down of strongholds. Eventually, as we are faithful, God will use our weapons of love, prayer, submission, God's Word, and the preaching of the cross. The stronghold will be assaulted and pulled down to the glory of God.

But, what then? Continuing the Roman army pattern,

we must take everyone captive for the glory of God. We must make every convert a thorough disciple of Christ:

* No more rebellion . . . no more self-rule!

* Our thoughts must become the thoughts of God because "as he thinketh in his heart, so is he" (Prov. 23:7).

* Our minds must be renewed in order that we may be transformed into the Lord's image (Rom. 12:2).

* We must teach the captive "all things" whatsoever Christ has commanded us (Matt. 28:20).

In other words, the objective of the warfare is to thoroughly win a convert to Jesus Christ. All of us began our lives as "children of disobedience" (Eph. 2:2). Jesus sought us (Luke 19:10), and used soul-winners to win us (Prov. 11:30). Our strongholds (each of us had excuses!) were overcome by godly persons utilizing superior spiritual weapons. It is our desire to submit to the obedience of Christ all that we are and have.

Remember, you are in a spiritual warfare! Put on your gospel armor each day (Eph. 6:10-17). Keep your offensive weapons ready and sharpened that you may "war a good warfare" (1 Tim. 1:18).

10
The Thorn in the Flesh

2 Corinthians 12:1-10

One of the most sacred—and spectacular—experiences of my life happened late one night. I was awakened from my sleep and stayed awake all night long. Perceiving the awakening to be of God, I went into a darkened living room and fell to my knees. I began to praise God and found myself raising my hands. I had never done this before, and soon I felt simply wonderful praising the Lord. As my hands went up (and they felt so heavy!), I felt myself going down and becoming more humble. Words are simply inadequate in expressing the joy of the Lord that night! I did not speak in an ecstatic language or shout aloud. There was a sense of God's Presence that filled and thrilled my soul.

We approach 2 Corinthians with much respect and reverence. Paul was willing to share a high honor and a sacred hour with us from his experience. He had been listing in chapter 11 the reasons and proofs of his apostleship. We might call this list the physical *servings* and *sufferings*. These would more than qualified Paul as an apostle. We now receive a final criterion for apostleship: spiritual visions and revelations.

This is a most controversial passage before us. We will divide it into three parts: *Paul's Experience* (vv. 1-6), *Satan's Emissary* (vv. 7-8), and *God's Explanation* (9-10).

Paul's Experience

Paul shares with us in verses 1-6 a once-in-Christianity happening! We are not sure when it happened. Some believe Paul had this ecstatic experience during his waiting years following his conversion: somewhere between Acts 9:30 and 11:25. Quite a few feel this could have happened at Lystra in Acts 14:19. We remember that Paul was stoned by his enemies and dragged out of the city. His adversaries thought he was dead. However, we note the miraculous reviving of Paul's spirit when the disciples gathered around him. Did Paul die and then come back alive? Today we hear reports of people's experiences on the operating table after being pronounced dead. A sensation of the person apart from the body has been described by many. Paul's experience happened during that miraculous resuscitation at Lystra.

In considering the experience of Paul, let us note several key points:

1. *Perplexity*—Note, first of all, Paul's choice of words in describing his experience. Out of humility, he used the third person several times: "I knew a man."

Further, realize that Paul was perplexed as to whether he was in the body or in a disembodied state during his experience. He wrote: "Whether in the body, or out of the body, I cannot tell" (vv. 2-3). He said this twice to emphasize his consternation as to whether he went to heaven physically or spiritually. Personally, I believe Paul's body was in Lystra, but the person of Paul went to paradise. This proves a person does not require a body to be conscious.

2. *Paradise*—Paul states that he was "caught up." This word means to be transferred, transported, or translated. Two other times in the New Testament this word is used:

(1) Acts 8:39 - where the Spirit of the Lord caught Philip and took him away from the presence of the Ethiopian eunuch. (2) 1 Thessalonians 4:17 - this passage dealing with Christ's coming tells how the saved on earth will be "caught up" and transported to heaven. In both cases the meaning is to move from one place to another. In Paul's experience, he was transported from this earth to another place.

Notice that Paul said he was caught up to the "third heaven" (v. 2). Over the years the idea has been that the air immediately above the earth is the first heaven. The stratosphere, the place of spaceships and planets, forms the second heaven. The third heaven is the habitation of God.

Paul said he was "caught up into paradise" (v. 4). The word "*paradise*" is a Persian word written in the Greek and means "royal garden." Two other times this word is found in the New Testament: (1) The dying thief was told by Jesus: "Today shalt thou be with me in paradise" (Luke 23:43). (2) The church at Ephesus (Rev. 2:7) was told that the overcomer would eat from the tree of life which is in the midst of paradise. We infer from these references, then, that paradise is a literal and lovely place. It is also equated with the third heaven. Paul went to the literal, lovely place of paradise.

3. *Preview*—Could this be a preview of what happens to us at death? At death the real person is transported from the body to the spiritual world of God. Death releases us from our body and places us in the presence of Christ: "absent from the body, and . . . present with the Lord" (2 Cor. 5:8).

We note in verse 4 that Paul heard "unspeakable words." Did Paul hear heavenly conversation between the angels? Did he overhear Jesus and His Father talking? Did God speak to him and share precious information about future happenings? We do not know because Paul would never speak specifically of it.

Paul's experience makes the unseen world more real and certain to us. Heaven seems more vivid to me when I realize Paul had this marvelous experience. He would be able to say later: "Eye hath not seen, nor ear heard, neither have entered into the heart of man, the things which God hath prepared for them that love him" (1 Cor. 2:9). He also would remind us that our affliction now is nothing to be compared to the future glory awaiting us (2 Cor. 4:17). Life after death was more certain and inviting to Paul after this wonderful experience.

Satan's Emissary

Paul had an unbelievably wonderful experience that was a once-in-Christianity event. Today, guess what would happen if someone claimed to have such an experience. At the very least, it would be publicized and marketed beyond description. Maybe even a new denomination would be founded upon it!

We come to that part of our passage concerning the thorn in the flesh. Let us note several points concerning the thorn:

1. *Prohibition*—The thorn in the flesh was, first of all, a prohibition. After that thrilling experience Paul may have been tempted to be "exalted above measure." God had a purpose for allowing Paul to have a paradise experience. However, lest the results of the experience go beyond God's purpose, Satan was allowed to implant a thorn. The thorn became a prohibition to Paul.

Every believer has experienced wonderful times in the

Lord. We have seen how Satan can use periods of exhilaration to produce pride. When we succumb to pride, we lower our guard, and Satan can send a fiery dart through an opening in our gospel armor. Verse 7 states the thorn was a prohibition lest Paul should be "exalted above measure."

2. *Physical*—The thorn was a physical affliction, not a spiritual crisis in Paul's life. Note in verse 7 that it is called a thorn in the *flesh*.

Several possibilities have been suggested as to the exact nature of the thorn: (1) spiritual temptation; (2) persecuting opposition—possibly the Judaizers; (3) carnal lust; (4) malaria—many of the physical symptoms are similar; (5) severe headaches; (6) epilepsy—physical symptoms are similar, also; (7) eye problems—ophthalmia has been mentioned using Galatians 4:14-15 and 6:11 as references.

It is providential that we do not know the specific nature of Paul's thorn. It is enough that we know that it was physical.

3. *Painful*—The affliction is called a "thorn." The word could be translated "stake" and refer to the painful custom where criminals were impaled. We think even of the painful crucifixion.

Paul pointed out that Satan used the thorn to "buffet" him. This word means to hit or strike with the hand, to slap. Satan would hit the apostle with this experience again and again. The pain was agonizing and incurable.

Much is said in the Bible concerning pain and suffering. The retributive suffering of the unbeliever is mentioned. Punitive suffering pays a people for their wrongdoing. Corrective suffering can happen when a child is corrected by his or her parents. Vicarious suffering takes place when one pays for another's sins. Educative suffering is endured to prove someone—this is suffering for a purpose as describing our Lord in Hebrews 5:8. We believe Paul's pain through the thorn in the flesh was educative pain. He was being prepared for further service through this experience.

4. *Prayer*—The physical pain prompted Paul to pray. In verse 8 we note several facts about Paul's prayer: (1) specific - he prayed specifically that it might be removed. Our prayers certainly should be specific: "Ye have not, because ye ask not" (Jas. 4:2). (2) Repeated - Paul said he made this request to the Lord three times. Personally, I feel he "really got through" three times! Certainly our prayers should be repeated—we should never cease praying. (3) Fervent - Paul "besought" or pleaded with the Lord in prayer. His prayer was not nonchalant or "ho hum." My father used to say, based on his experiences during World War II as a medic, that there were no atheists in foxholes!" When the bullets started flying, and one realized his name could be on the next one—the soldier prayed! And he made contact! Paul's prayer was fervent, and he made clear contact with God three times.

Paul's prayers were not answered in the affirmative, however, and that brings us to our next point:

God's Explanation

There used to be a popular television commercial where two men were talking about their financial brokers. All talk in the crowded place would cease when one of the men stated: "My broker is E. F. Hutton, and E. F. Hutton says . . . "

Paul could pray as no other Christian. Why wasn't the great man of God's prayer answered? All talk ceases as we listen reverently for God's explanation. Three parts are needed to explain God's answer:

1. *Purpose*—Paul prayed for the specific removal of the thorn. God provided Paul with something better than the removal of the thorn. Paul was given a revelation!

Through the experience of the thorn, Paul was given a revelation about himself. He saw that he had the potential to be a proud person. He needed that thorn to discipline him in a dangerous area of life. The thorn revealed Paul's true character.

Through the experience of the thorn, Paul was given a revelation of the nature of pain. He came to know how much he could stand by way of physical suffering. Now he could sympathize with others who endured great physical pain. Paul knew that God would be with him, and His grace would be sufficient to carry Paul through this trial and any trial.

Through the experience of the thorn, Paul was given a revelation of the character of God. God is faithful. God is loving and will not put more on us than we can bear. Paul came to realize that nothing would ever happen to him that he and God could not handle together.

What would have happened if God had answered Paul's prayer and had ended the trial? Paul would have been deprived of claiming God's sufficient grace. We would have been so much poorer in our knowledge of the way God deals with His children. There was a sense of purpose in God's explanation.

2. *Power*—God explained to Paul that the trial would remain but would be accompanied by His enduring grace. Paul would be given supernatural power to endure the thorn! God's Presence brought grace and power to Paul's life.

Have you ever wondered what you would do if certain

trials came into your life? I have often wondered how I would die: Would I be faithful? Afraid? Then I realized that the dying grace would not be given to me until I needed it! Supernatural grace was given to Paul when he needed it and not before. This experience tells us that when we need the powerful grace of God, it will be there! There seems to be three areas of grace: saving grace, living grace, and dying grace. Each one will be ready for you when you need to draw from it.

3. *Pleasure*—There was another lesson Paul learned from God's answer, and it involved his attitude. Our experiences can either make us or break us. We can become better or bitter by our attitudes toward experiences in life. Do we really believe God is a loving God who has our best interest at heart? Do we truly trust that God has a wonderful purpose for our lives? As we learn to go through life's experiences trusting our Heavenly Father, we reach an attitude of pleasure concerning trials.

Knowing that God had a purpose for each trial, Paul's attitude was one of pleasure. Knowing that God would not put more on him than he could bear, Paul's attitude was one of pleasure. Knowing that God would be with him during the trial, Paul's attitude was one of pleasure. Paul's preference, more than anything, was the will of God. He did not have a fatalistic attitude of: what will be, will be. Nor did Paul have an attitude of resistance as experiences came. As God's will developed into Paul's life, he took pleasure because that would be best for him.

In verse 10, Paul gave a list that seems comprehensive for all experiences in life. Paul expected personal weaknesses, financial difficulties, persecution, and unstoppable distresses. He knew they were coming because they came to Christ's followers in every age. We should expect the same.

The coming crises are inevitable. The key is our attitude toward the thorn in the flesh. When God's will is our goal, our complaining is changed to contentment. Our worrying will be exchanged for worshiping. We will do less groaning and more glorying!

In closing, let me share several foundational principles from this passage:

* Christians should pray for relief from bodily pain and expect God to bring deliverance.

* If God does not bring deliverance, He has a purpose and will give sustaining grace.

* Pain can be endured with patience because grace will be granted. This grace will not be received until it is needed.

* The sufferers will find God's power in their lives as they yield totally to the Lord.

11
Self-Examination

2 Corinthians 13:5-6

Have you ever considered what a "test"-conscious world we live in? All of us have been given many tests thus far in our lives. No matter the level one achieves in business, it seems there will always be a battery of tests to be taken.

Our high school seniors must take the SAT or the ACT to gain college entrance. College seniors must go through further tests in order to enter graduate school. Accountants must take their CPA. To be a real-estate salesperson, one must pass a strenuous examination. All of us should be thankful that each person driving a car must pass several tests! Even our homes are given tests for radon and aluminum. And now there are at-home tests where people can examine themselves for pregnancy and cancer.

The apostle Paul proposed a very interesting test to the members of the Corinthian church: "Examine yourselves, whether ye be in the faith; prove your own selves" (2 Cor. 13:5). The most feared words to my ears in college and graduate school were: "Take out a clean sheet of paper. This is a pop test." I still flinch upon remembering those words coming from my professors! Paul's test, however, was not a "pop test." This would be an open-book test. The

Corinthians had been examining Paul's credentials of apostolic validity. Now, he turned the tables on them, suggesting they themselves take a test concerning their faith in Christ and faithfulness to Him.

Notice in verses 3-7 the number of times "prove" is mentioned. Paul used a word which means to put to the test or to determine if genuine or real. As a matter of fact, even the word *reprobate* comes from this same word and means tried and found worthless, counterfeit, or discredited after a test. Paul was assured of his position and relationship in Jesus Christ. He challenged them to examine themselves about their faith in the gospel.

This is an interesting thought: giving yourself a test to determine your relationship to Christ. May I suggest a sevenfold test to examine one's place in Christ?

Conversion Test

The most important test in a person's life is the one that determines his relationship to God through Jesus Christ. One may have high marks in other areas of life, but if he fails here, "good were it for that man if he had never been born" (Mark 14:21). "For what shall it profit a man, if he shall gain the whole world, and lose his own soul? Or what shall a man give in exchange for his soul?" (Mark 8:36-37). This is the most important test of a human life: the conversion test.

Have you ever been converted? Have you passed from death to life? Do you know beyond a shadow of doubt that, if you died, you would go to Heaven? Have you repented of your sins (Luke 13:3)? Have you ever received Jesus Christ (John 1:12)? Have you ever called upon the name of the Lord (Rom. 10:13)? It is possible to know whether or not you have been converted: "Hereby know we that we dwell in him, and he in us, because he hath given us of his

Spirit" (1 John 4:13). If any do not have the Spirit of Christ, they are "none of his" (Rom. 8:9). Salvation is a personal experience that no one can doubt: either he or she has or has not opened the door (Rev. 3:20).

I have a seven-year-old son, Daniel, who was saved recently. During our revival, I took him home one afternoon after school. He begged me to stay home and play ball with him. "Daniel, I can't stay home because I have to go visiting," I said.

Daniel replied, "Daddy, you don't really have to go visiting."

"Oh, yes I do," I stated. "If daddy doesn't visit people, they won't walk forward." To which Daniel gave this profound testimony: "Nobody visited me, and I went forward. I just felt it!"

The language of the seven-year-old may not be perfect, but the message is plain: salvation is a real experience, and we know when it happens. What about the conversion test in your life?

Character Test

Salvation is a spiritual birth (John 3:3; 1 Pet. 1:23). When one is physically born, one inherits the characteristics of parents and other relatives. At the birth of our son, my wife exclaimed, "Oh, he has the Tallant ears!" That little crinkle in his ear is a family characteristic and identifies Daniel as coming from the Friel and Tallant families.

At conversion, we inherit the nature of our Heavenly Father. As we grow, we become more like Him. You have seen the resemblance even between husbands and wives. As they spend years together, they begin to look and act like each other. I think it is phenomenal when even their dog begins to look like them! As we grow in Christ, we begin to "bear the image of the heavenly" (1 Cor. 15:49). The due process of the spiritual nature is for Christ to be formed in us (Gal. 4:19).

What will we look like as the resemblance to our Heavenly Father begins to take place? Notice the fruit of the Spirit in Galatians 5:22-23: "love, joy, peace, long-suffering, gentleness, goodness, faith, meekness, temperance." As we walk in the Spirit, the nature of God as seen in the fruit of the Holy Spirit will be produced in us.

I take it as a genuine compliment when old timers tell me: "As long as you are alive, people will not forget George Mays!" George Mays was my grandfather, and I look more like him than even my own father. We have personality traits that are strikingly similar. His nature is in mine. Some experts believe we receive more from the entry of our grandparents' nature than from our own parents. What about your spiritual character? Do you resemble your Heavenly Father? Do your works "glorify your Father which is in heaven?" (Matt. 5:16).

Continuation Test

Our country has over one million runaway children each year. We are also seeing "drop-out" parents who forsake the responsibility of the home. A most revealing test for the Christian is the continuation test. Someone has said that if "one's faith fizzles before the finish, then there was a flaw at the first!" Our denominational leaders are alarmed at the number of members who cannot be found. Many are not scoring well on the continuation test. On practically any given Sunday in the year, less than 50 percent of our denomination's members will be present for Bible study

Paul told Timothy, "Continue thou in the things which thou hast learned and hast been assured of" (2 Tim. 3:14).

How is your continuance? Are you growing in the grace and knowledge of our Lord and Savior Jesus Christ? (2 Pet. 3:18). I have seen Christians drop out of Christian fellowship and service for years! Some may be offended because of tribulation or persecution (Matt. 13:21). Others have the word choked through the care of this world and the deceitfulness of riches (Matt. 13:22). All of us have seen outstanding church leaders drop out of fellowship and service. How this grieves us leaders. How it must break God's heart!

It is not God's fault if we do not pass the continuation test! "Whatsoever is born of God overcometh the world" (1 John 5:4). We have the victory in us, even our faith which overcomes the world. We know that God is constantly working in us giving us the desire and the ability to do his good pleasure (Phil. 2:13). We cannot blame God for not passing the continuation test.

Companion Test

At salvation the child of God begins to experience a sense of family. Before I was saved, I frequently was seen in the company of the unsaved, the rude and crude, and even the reprobate. A miracle took place after my salvation, however, and I began to gravitate toward God's people. I found that one of the evidences of my salvation was: "We know that we have passed from death unto life, because we love the brethren" (1 John 3:14). I cannot explain it, but I simply became uncomfortable around those who cursed, told dirty jokes, and had no interest in God.

A famous basketball player once gave his testimony about being around people experimenting with drugs. He said that, when he came into a room and realized drugs were being used, he immediately began his "fast break" toward the door! Amen! Righteousness has no fellowship with unrighteousness. Light has no union with darkness.

I found 1 Peter 4:2-4 to be absolutely true! We should not live the rest of our time in the flesh but to the will of God. We may have walked in times past in revelings, banquetings, excess of wine—but now, no more! The Bible is so true when it says that "they think it strange that ye run not with them to the same excess of riot, speaking evil of you" (1 Pet. 4:4). We are not the same anymore. We can be friendly with the world but not have fellowship with it. We are interested in the world but can no longer be intimate with it. We are in daily contact with the world but cannot enjoy communion with it.

What about your companion test? Do you still enjoy being around the same old, unsaved crowd? Remember that Jesus' family came after Him one day to take Him back home. The crowd told Jesus that His mother and brothers were out there. Jesus said, "Whosoever shall do the will of God, the same is my brother, and my sister, and mother" (Mark 3:35). I am certain you have found that your spiritual family is more meaningful to you than your unsaved or worldly earthly family.

Currency Test

Very possibly one of the popular tests Jesus used to examine people was the currency test. The majority of Jesus' parables used the theme of stewardship. What a person thinks of his currency is a revealing test of discipleship. We remember that the "love of money is the root of all evil" (1 Tim. 6:10). Many of the commandments are broken because of the love of money. Failing in the currency test causes one to err from the faith with the result of being pierced by many sorrows.

An outstanding golf star recently purchased a limited-edition automobile for over $200,000. He said that the car would not be driven but left parked in his basement. Today it is not enough to buy clothing to fit our needs. It must be designer clothing! Many of us have our "treasures upon earth" and are worshiping corruptible gods that have no eternal value. Jesus said, "For where your treasure is, there will your heart be also" (Matt. 6:21).

Where is your treasure? How do you rate in the currency test? Are you faithful in giving the Lord the firstfruit? Begin the life of obedient stewardship today by starting to tithe and give offerings.

Crisis Test

When trouble comes, to what or whom do you turn? Before salvation I tended to depend upon my ingenuity, my abilities, and my strength. I never thought of prayer or seeking the Lord's will from His Word. Again, it was mysterious as I found myself crying "Abba, Father" when crises came after salvation. My wife had a young lady in her Sunday School class who found Jesus. She had led a rough life and received no support at home from an unsaved husband. Ann soon had to have a serious surgery, and my wife taught her how to pray, to seek God's answer in the Scriptures, and to get other Christians praying. The surgery was successful to the amazement of the doctors. This new babe in Christ proclaimed in her testimony: "For the first time in my life I finally did something right!" The crisis test was passed victoriously.

Examine yourself concerning the crisis test. Are you fearful? a worrier? Experts tell us that most of our fears never come to pass. We never saw Goliath throw a punch! He scared the Israelites by his words until David came on the scene full of confidence in God. Listen! "God hath not given us the spirit of fear; but of power, and of love, and of a sound mind" (2 Tim. 1:7).

Once an elderly woman spent some time in the hospital with pains, none of which were critical. The family gathered around her, and her daughter said, "Mother, the doctor has done all he can. You'll have to trust God for the rest." A look of hopelessness came over the face of the aged lady and she exclaimed, "Oh, dear, has it come to that?" Yes! We should always be trusting God with our lives. The crises' tests will certainly come. We must be in the Word daily, committing all to Him in prayer, and knowing He will not put more on us than we can bear. Oh, yes, Romans 8:28 is still in the Book!

Concern Test

The final test is a revealing one: concern for others. The first disciples were beaten and threatened if they spoke again in Jesus' name. Remember Peter's answer? " We cannot but speak the things which we have seen and heard" (Acts 4:20). There was a concern in the disciples for other people that defied the threat of physical harm! "Whosoever believeth on him shall not be ashamed" (Rom. 10:11).

How would you rate yourself on the concern test? When was the last time you shared your faith with someone? John asked this probing question of us: How can people love God whom they have not seen when they do not love their brothers whom they have seen? The answer was given when John said that persons who love God will love their brothers and sisters also (1 John 4:21). Once I led a sweet young girl to place her faith in Jesus Christ. Amid much weeping, the girl prayed for Jesus to come into her heart. Almost in the next breath she prayed for her lost father! Praise God! To me, that is an evidence of salvation because the "love of God is shed abroad in our hearts by the Holy Ghost which is given unto us" (Rom. 5:5).

Studies indicate that the longer a person is a Christian the fewer lost people he or she knows. That is good and bad! The key, however, lies in the fact that God brings us into contact with opportunities for witness every day. We must be ready to give a reason of the hope that lies in us. We should be instant in season and out of season to share the Word. Are you like Jeremiah? "Then I said, I will not make mention of him, nor speak any more in his name. But his word was in mine heart as a burning fire shut up in my bones, and I was weary with forbearing, and I could not stay" (Jer. 20:9). May God lead us to be concerned about those around us without Christ.

You have seen the test: conversion, character, continuation, companion, currency, crisis, and concern. How did you score? "Examine yourselves, whether ye be in the faith; prove your own selves."

12
Firm Facts About the Future

2 Corinthians 5:1-8

Have you discovered the importance of a reservation? One of the most agonizing nights of my life happened when my wife and I were seminary students in New Orleans. We were taking a week's vacation at Christmastime and were heading to Orlando, Florida, from New Orleans. I was pushing to get more miles under my belt before stopping for the night. As Marilynn urged me to stop, I kept saying, "One more exit. The more we do tonight, the less travel tomorrow."

Finally, I reluctantly pulled off to a motel only to hear the clerk say: "Sorry, sir, we're full. This is a rough time of the year to find a decent motel without a reservation." How prophetic that proved to be! Motel after motel—filled to capacity with Christmas travelers! I received firsthand a spiritual "deja vu" based on Luke 2:7! Joseph had his Mary, and I had my Marilynn, but the answer was still the same: "no room for them in the inn." Sometime late in the evening and somewhere across the Florida line, I found an off-brand motel with a room left for a weary, foolish traveler. I had learned a lesson, however, that has stuck with me to this day: make sure about your reservation!

The apostle Paul had been honest with the Corinthian

church about the difficulties of life. In the previous chapter he mentioned troubles, perplexities, persecutions, and sufferings. Paul called them "light affliction" (v. 17), but they are still affliction!

With his honesty Paul wanted also to emphasize the hope of the church. Paul had the highest of hopes for the church based on the certainties of the resurrection and eternal glory. Notice the language of certainties Paul used in describing the invisible world and the otherwise unknown eternity ahead for the church:

"We know" - verses 1 and 6

"We have" - verse 1 - present possession

"We are confident" - verses 6 and 8

This language of certainties is based on revelation faith. The apostle had been inspired by God to share firm facts about the future with the church. The church needs hope to face the uncertainties of life and the certainties of an unknown and intimidating future.

Paul gave hope to the church by announcing: "God has a reservation for you. You are expected, and you have a place to stay." Two mothers of teenagers were talking. One said: "My daughter doesn't tell me anything. I'm a nervous wreck." The other mother exclaimed: "My daughter tells me everything. I'm a nervous wreck!" Such appears to be the state of many Christians: not knowing about the future worries them, and knowing about the future frightens them.

I have been with many people who have severe sicknesses. Not once have I heard a person say to the doctor: "Please, Doctor, do not tell me my true condition. I just don't think I could stand it!" People want to know the facts, so they can prepare. We are made "wise unto salvation" by knowing God's Word (2 Tim. 3:15). Even though

Jesus said: "It is not for you to know the times or the seasons, which the Father hath put in his own power" (Acts 1:7), there are some firm facts about the future which we may know. Using 2 Corinthians 5:1-8, let us be encouraged by knowing these firm facts:

Firm Fact # 1: All Christians Will Not Die

My grandparents had a huge trailer park in Central Florida. As a boy I played there practically every day. One day an old German lady moved into the park, and we became close friends. Although I was not yet a Christian, I was thrilled to know that she was a retired missionary. How we talked about God and His Word! I believe the most startling fact she ever shared with me was the fact that I may never die. Miss Mizner encouraged me to cultivate the hope of Christ's coming. I grew into my present manhood cherishing the possibility that I may be alive when Jesus Christ returns.

Paul was not totally sure he would die. He said: "For we know that *if* our earthly house of this tabernacle were dissolved" (2 Cor. 5:1, italics mine). The apostle is saying that, if this body in which we live collapses or falls to pieces, we have an eternal body in heaven. This present tent may not wear out and may carry us to the time of Jesus' Return. Paul gave us this firm fact in other writings:

* 1 Corinthians 15:51: "Behold, I show you a mystery; We shall *not all sleep*, but we shall all be changed" (italics mine). "Sleep" is often used for the Christian death. When Jesus comes, Paul says, not all Christians will have to be resurrected. Some will be alive on the earth.

* 1 Thessalonians 4:17: - "Then we which are *alive* and remain shall be caught up together with them in the clouds, to meet the Lord in the air: and so shall we ever be

with the Lord" (italics mine). Again, Paul's words point us to the return of Christ. He related the details of the resurrection of the already dead saints in verse 16. Then he said, "We which are alive and remain"—there will be those saved on the earth when Our Lord returns. You may be one of them!

Firm fact #1: "All Christians will not die." Paul gave some counsel for those who may not experience death:

1. Be prepared: we do not want to be found "naked" (2 Cor. 5:3). "Naked" could mean unprepared (without clothing). We must all be prepared for death or the Lord's return (Amos 4:12).

2. Walk by faith and not by sight (v. 7). Believe the Bible (Rom. 10:17). Govern your life by the revelation of God's Word.

3. Continue to labor and serve (v. 9). Wear out for the Lord, don't rust out! Let us be found faithful serving our Lord.

4. Be a witness to others (vv. 11,14). Whether the terror of the Lord (v. 11) or the love of Christ (v. 14), we should share Christ with others. The only thing from earth that will be in heaven will be people! Share that others may live eternally.

Firm Fact # 2: All Christians Have an Eternal Home

Hopefully, we established the principle in Firm Fact #1 that all Christians will not die. However, what happens when a believer *does die*? Life after death is of grave concern to everyone: from little children to senior adults. Until people settle the eternity question, they cannot live the abundant life Jesus wants for them (John 10:10).

Ignorance about eternal life can make people miserable. I believe one of the saddest commentaries I have ever experienced came from the lips of a young boy. This youngster's father passed away suddenly with a heart attack. The man was in the prime of life and the central figure in that home. Both mother and son worshiped the father and depended upon him totally. Shock and confusion followed in the wake of the dad's death. A few weeks later, the mother and son were driving down the highway when the boy said: "Mother, why don't you just pull over there and hit the ditch? You can't take care of me. You can't even take care of yourself. When we die, we'll go to heaven, and Daddy will then take care of us both!" The mother was absolutely speechless at her son's remarks.

Paul communicated hope to the Corinthian church as he gave firm fact #2: all Christians have an eternal home. Death was described by Paul as a "dissolving" of the earthly body: this is a picture of a tent being dismantled. The earthly body is like a tent (*skenous* from *skene*, a tent, from *ska*, to cover). The real person is carried about in this life by the flesh-and-blood body which is likened to a tabernacle or tent. There is vivid Old Testament imagery here as we remember the tabernacle symbolically housed the Presence of God. Paul said that, when *this* earthly house is taken down by death, the Christian will be given a new body. This body is eternal and will never get tired or wear out. God Himself is the architect of this heavenly body.

For the children of God to live eternally, their bodies will have to be changed. This frail, mortal, earthly body will have to undergo a miraculous transformation to a supernatural body equipped to live eternally. In our passage, Paul used descriptive phrases like: "clothed upon with our house which is from heaven" (v. 2) and "mortality might be swallowed up of life" (v. 4). We wish our temporary earthly body to be covered over by a heavenly body.

A man was fishing one day when he heard a woman scream for help. The hero paddled to where the woman thrashed about in the lake and tried to pull her into his boat. He grabbed her arm, but it was artificial and pulled off. He next grabbed her by the hair but lost her because she was wearing a wig. In desperation, he put his finger into her mouth, the way one would boat a fish. But, this didn't work either because she was wearing false teeth. This prompted the man to holler: "Somebody come help me save as much of this woman as we can!"

What comfort to know the Christian will receive a new heavenly body from God. The new body will have all eternal parts! You will want to read 1 Corinthians 15:35-58 to find out more about our resurrection bodies. Our old bodies are characterized as corrupt, dishonorable, weak, natural, and earthly. The new house from heaven will be incorruptible, glorious, powerful, spiritual, and heavenly. The change will take place in about the fastest movement Paul could describe: the "twinkling of an eye" (v. 52). Jesus, our Savior, is the Prototype: He is the 'firstfruits of them that slept" (vv. 20,22-23). Our eternal bodies will be like Jesus' resurrection body (1 John 3:2).

Often when a young college athlete receives a great financial package for signing with a professional football team, the first thing he buys is a new house for his parents. He wants them to have a better home in which to live. Paul gave us a firm fact for the future: God is expecting you, and you will be given a perfect place in which to live throughout eternity.

Firm Fact # 3: Fellowship with Christ Is Forever

Have you ever heard: "Out of sight, out of mind"? This third firm fact for the future can be illustrated by the way children treat "out of sight, out of mind." Have you ever witnessed a parent trying to leave a child in the church nursery for the first time? Oh, what a scene! Crying, screaming, and agony on everyone! It is as if the child feels that, when the parents walk around the corner, they are gone forever. This is why "Peek-A-Boo" games are good for children.

Every child of God desires that security knowing their Heavenly Father will always be there for them. I believe we have produced the most confused, anxious generation of children in the history of the earth. Absentee parents, broken homes, latchkey children, orphans—the security of a home for a child has been denied this generation. A little boy in our Christian School was a terror to the students, teachers, and the administration. Wild behavior and poor grades characterized his school performance. Upon speaking to the parent, I found that this boy only recently was adopted. He had been given up by his real parents and had been passed around until this godly family found him. I shall not ever forget something the adopted mother said: "His adoption to us should be final any day. I believe all will settle down when he realizes he will never have to leave us."

"Never have to leave": Christians have a firm fact for the future when they realize God will never leave them or forsake them (Heb. 13:5). What wonderful words in 1 Thessalonians 4:17: "So shall we *ever* be with the Lord" (italics mine). No wonder Paul said in the next verse: "Wherefore *comfort* one another with these words" (italics mine).

Paul shows that we are "with" Christ from now on. While in this earthly body, we walk by faith and enjoy the Lord's Presence. And, when we "absent" the body, we will be perfectly "present with the Lord" (v. 8). This reminds us of Philippians 1:21: "For me to live is Christ, and to die is gain." Our sure fact is that our relationship with Christ will never end.

Firm Fact # 4: God Gives a Sure Guarantee

Have you ever heard old timers speak of how business transactions were done, especially land deals? As the contract was being finalized, the present owner would hand the purchaser a bag full of earth taken from the intended purchase. This would be a part of the intended full-purchased possession. The rest would be his when all the money was paid.

Concerning our future, Paul said that God "hath given unto us the earnest of the Spirit" (v. 5). Paul used a word for "earnest," *arrhabon*, which refers to a part payment on a total obligation. An earnest is a pledge binding a bargain. It is something given or done as an indication or assurance of what is to come. If you have purchased a home recently, as I have, you no doubt have heard the expression: "earnest money."

One of our firm facts about the future is the giving of the Holy Spirit as our guarantee of the heavenly inheritance. Please note the salvation process found in Ephesians 1:12-14:

1. We must *hear* the "word of truth" or gospel (v. 13).
2. We believe or trust the "word of truth" or gospel (v. 13).
3. Then "salvation" is wrought (v. 13).
4. We are "sealed" with the Holy "Spirit of promise" (v. 13).

5. The Holy Spirit is given as an "earnest of our inheritance" (v. 14).

6. There is the "redemption of the purchased possession" (v. 14).

At salvation, the Holy Spirit is given to people (1 Cor. 6:19). The Holy Spirit, upon taking up His residence within us, is the divine Witness that we are God's. The Spirit is also the pledge, deposit, or guarantee of our complete inheritance. What God has given already to us in part, He will bestow at last in perfection. In the Spirit, we have a little piece of heaven to go to heaven with.

When was the last time God reminded you that you are His and that He has a place reserved for you?

* Was it when the Holy Spirit gave you a revelation from the Word of God? —a truth exactly for that moment?

* Was it when the Holy Spirit led you in a certain situation?—gave you guidance to make a decision? (Rom. 8:14).

* Was it the ripening of spiritual fruit: love, joy, peace, longsuffering, gentleness, goodness, faith, meekness, or temperance? (Gal. 5:22-23)? You're looking more like Christ.

* Was it a thrilling realization of His Presence during a worship experience, public or personal? Like Jacob, you felt this place was God's house, and you did not realize it (Gen. 28:16-17)?

May God help us acknowledge and appreciate those times when He reminds us that we are His and that we have an inheritance awaiting us in Glory.

Firm Fact # 5: There Is a Heavenly Desire

Have you ever seen a young couple on the verge of purchasing a new house? They have been living in a small apartment with all the usual problems: rough area, high rent, awful neighbors, and poor upkeep by the management. God works everything out as they even draw their own plans for the house. The loan is worked out with the bank. The contractors are finished, and, even though the grass is still covered by straw, they are about to move into their new house! What a day!

This is the way the apostle Paul felt about the claiming of his home in heaven. He was ready to go! He had worked hard in serving the Lord. His body felt the years of toil and suffering. More and more earth did not seem to be home to him. He could feel the tug of heaven upon his soul.

Without appearing too prejudiced, I assert that I am a satisfied citizen of the state of Tennessee! I was born in Ohio and appreciate it because God chose that state for my birth. I was reared in Florida and thank God for my childhood and teen experiences preparing me for manhood. I received my Bible and ministry training in Louisiana and praise God for using that state in preparing me to be a pastor. However, I do not wish to go back to Ohio, Florida, or Louisiana! After being anywhere else for a while, I start hankering for Tennessee! I know Tennessee pastors who simply could not adjust when they left this state. I've even felt the tug of Tennessee when I was in Jerusalem, Israel! (and I guess you don't get any closer to God than in Jesus' own country!).

Paul was feeling heaven's tugs. He said: "For in this we *groan, earnestly desiring* to be clothed upon with our house which is from heaven" (2 Cor. 5:2, italics mine). Paul was getting homesick for Glory. As long as God had a purpose for him, he would stay. But, if God desired for him to leave, Paul was ready (Phil. 1:22-24). There used to be a popular song with the theme: the best is always yet to come. The song traced the joys of childhood, youth, young adult years with family, median adult years with vocation joys, and senior adult years in retirement. At each stage, the best was always yet to come. I believe that! Don't you hear God saying: "Don't worry. The best is yet to be."

A little boy was flying a kite when darkness fell. He remained outside for a while, sitting on the curb, holding the string. A man came by and asked the boy what he was doing. "I'm flying a kite," replied the boy. The man looked up into the dark sky and said, "How do you know you're still flying a kite?" The boy profoundly answered: "Because I can feel the tug on the other end!" As we get older and more prepared for heaven, we will feel the tug on the other end. Are you homesick for heaven?

Wanting to lift the hopes of the Corinthian church, Paul gave them five firm facts about the future. Let us close this chapter the way we began: reservations help us when traveling. We know we are expected in heaven and have a place to stay. Do you have your reservation?